Jaromír Šimonek
Coordination Abilities in Volleyball

Jaromír Šimonek

Coordination Abilities in Volleyball

—

Managing Editor: Konstantin Kougioumtzis

Language Editor: Deirdre Scully

Published by De Gruyter Open Ltd, Warsaw/Berlin.

This work is licensed under the Creative Commons Attribution-NonCommercial-NoDerivs 3.0 license, which means that the text may be used for non-commercial purposes, provided credit is given to the author. For details go to http://creativecommons.org/licenses/by-nc-nd/3.0/.

Copyright © 2014 Jaromir Simonek

ISBN 978-3-11-037030-0
e- ISBN 978-3-11-037031-7

Bibliographic information published by the Deutsche Nationalbibliothek
The Deutsche Nationalbibliothek lists this publication in the Deutsche Nationalbibliografie; detailed bibliographic data are available in the Internet at http://dnb.dnb.de.

Managing Editor: Konstantin Kougioumtzis
Language Editor: Deirdre Scully

www.degruyteropen.com

Cover illustration: © IStock/barsik

Contents

Introduction

1	Definitions and Description of Basic Terms —— 1	
1.1	Modelling the Sport Preparation in Volleyball —— 6	
1.2	Characteristics of the Sport Preparation in Sport Games —— 7	
2	Factors in the Structure of Performance in Sport Games —— 11	
3	Coordination Abilities and Their Impact on Sport Performance —— 15	
3.1	Definition and Structure of Coordination Abilities —— 17	
3.2	Relationship Between Coordination Abilities and Motor Skills —— 24	
3.3	Possibilities of Development of Coordination Abilities —— 27	
3.4	Methodology of Development of Coordination Abilities —— 29	
3.4.1	Methods and Organization of the Development of Coordination Abilities —— 30	
3.4.2	Methodical Hints to the Development of General and Special Coordination Abilities —— 31	
4	Age Dynamics and Intergender Differences in the Level of Coordination Abilities —— 32	
4.1	Peculiarities of the Development of Coordination Abilities at Ages 6-9 Years —— 34	
4.2	Peculiarities of Development of Coordination Abilities at the Age of 10-17 Years —— 37	
4.3	Age Peculiarities in the Development of Coordination Abilities at the Age of 18-22 Year —— 38	
5	System of Complex Control of the Level of Coordination Abilities —— 41	
5.1	Assessment of the Level of Coordination Abilities by Means of Performance Standards —— 42	
5.1.1	Tests of Coordination Abilities —— 43	
5.1.2	Using Standards and Tables —— 46	
6	Model of Development of Coordination Abilities in Long-term Sport Preparation in Volleyball —— 48	
6.1	Characteristics of Motor Activity in Colleyball —— 49	
6.2	Factors Limiting Sport Performance in Volleyball —— 51	
6.3	Periodization of the Contents of Sport Preparation in Volleyball —— 55	
6.4	Methodology of Development of Coordination Abilities in Volleyball —— 57	

Conclusions —— 70
References —— 71
Index —— 79

Introduction

Top sport nowadays is characterized by a high sports performance, perfect technique, exacting character of competitions, placing highest demands on motor, psychological and physiological aspects of an athlete´s personality. Thus, the questions of rational selection of young talented individuals for sport, as well as improvement of sports preparation, especially in its initial stages, have come to the forefront.

The core content of sports preparation gradually passes from quantity to quality. Trainers and coaches focus more on effective exploitation of training time, since the health of athletes will not tolerate further increases in the number and load of training units. The quality of sports training rests on the exploitation of "sensitive periods" for the development of motor prerequisites crucial for a given sport, as well as for the acquisition and improvement of motor skills fundamental to the improvement of motor performance regulation and perfecting movement coordination.

Models of long-term sports preparation which are based on a thorough analysis and generalization of latest instruction and experience from a wide spectrum of experts play an important role in providing high quality of sports preparation. Besides conditioning, the development of coordination abilities is considered to be an apparent component of sports preparation. In spite of this, no models exist of the development of coordination abilities which could form a good aid for coaches in sports schools and classes.

The aim of this work is to let trainers and coaches know how to use the model of coordination preparation in volleyball. When elaborating the model of long-term sports preparation with the focus on the development of coordination abilities we relied on the references available and results of finished experiments showing evidence of unequivocal similarities of coordination factors of the whole sports performance.

The task of this monograph is to submit several training programmes focused on the development of coordination abilities for the stage of initial sports preparation, initial specialization, as well as specialized sports preparation stage. Application of the abovementioned programmes should result in an improved motor display of a sportsperson, faster acquisition of motor skills, as well as higher percentage of effectiveness in a game.

The main method, which was used for the elaboration of the programmes, was the one of modelling. To reach sufficient data, the method of testing of coordination abilities of players, was used. The detailed description can be found in individual chapters describing models of development of coordination abilities in different sports games.

1 Definitions and Description of Basic Terms

Sports preparation itself represents a complex system of phenomena, connections and behaviour of its components. If we want to reach the goal of sports preparation – to nurture a top athlete able to reach an optimum performance in any conditions – we have to try, based on thorough knowledge of the individual and knowledge of specific age, sexual and developmental peculiarities, to create a model of rational long-term sports preparation which presupposes application of adequate and effective training means, methods and forms of work, optimum training loads and suitable frequency and follow-up in training cycles. To solve this crucial task for the trainer, the method of programming-modelling is used. To start to prepare a new model, it is practically necessary to define basic terms used in the book.

Modelling is a creative process resulting in the elaboration of optimum models. Through this, it is possible to describe phenomena and processes from the point of view of structure, functions, intentions of the course, as well as from the point of view of planning a possible and required development and final effect. The method is considered as one of the basic ways of investigating complex pedagogical phenomena as systems of intentional behaviour. The method of modelling is based on elaborating a model encompassing characteristic features of the personality of an athlete with levels of factors which limit sports performance in the given sport.

Modelling in sport is a creative process focused on designing optimum rational models of the long-term sports preparation, which also consider changes in athletes, developmental issues and external factors. The effect of model realization is on a higher level than the real model created by the input information. In sports, modelling is generally used in connection with:
- games modelling,
- modelling of conditions of games,
- working out models of long-term preparation, training units, micro-, mezo-, macro-cycles,
- modelling of characteristics of an ideal player,
- application of technical means and using of information (programmes of development of motor abilities, acquisition of rational sports technique and tactics).

A model is the result of the process of modelling and represents an idealized and materialized system which adequately reflects the object of investigation or analogously depicts its specific features and relations. In a broader sense, it represents an object deputizing other objects, which is able to offer information on them. A model presumes a precise notion of what factors and in which sequence such factors should be formed. It requires knowledge on how to create all the required features, abilities and skills determining the attainment of a top sporting performance. Moreover, it requires, an optimum contents, focus and progression of how to reach the final state in connection with the changes in individual factors of sports performance structure as to the age dynamism of their development. The development of individual factors should be planned in a rational way – through an optimum use of "sensitive periods", when the organism reacts to a specific training stimulus in the most optimum way and it is thus possible to reach the clearest changes during the shortest time (Šimonek, 1979).

Šimonek defines the model of an athlete as the picture of an ideal performer, a model depiction of ideal prerequisites of an athlete for reaching a certain performance goal. As a rule it includes information on somatic, motor, coordination-technical and personality prerequisites for reaching the set performance goal. From this point of view we can speak about a model of the talented performer – beginner, a model of the future Olympic winner, or a world record holder, but also an athlete of a certain performance level. Models of this kind have a great activating and motivating aim because they represent the target desired through sport preparation in volleyball.

Supposing that the models are as a rule oriented at final, target performances, from the point of view of the long-term sports preparation of young athletes, the so-called basal models are of greatest importance because they represent a sum of model characteristics of various aspects of preparedness of young sportspersons. At the end of the stage of expanded sports specialization in the selected sport, a young athlete should master a wide spectrum of motor habits and skills, reach a harmonious development of motor abilities – conditioning as well as coordination skills – inevitable for a successful specialization and transition into adulthood.

Modern science in sports training emphasises models in which the top level focuses on general and special physical preparation, technical and tactical mastery, while reaching the planned sports performance should be based on a fundamental basic functional and coordination preparation.

Table 1.1 shows the position of indicators of functional preparedness of a sportsperson according to the importance for the particular kind of sport. In sport games we can find analysers in the first level of importance, while in the second one these are functional systems of the organism. It is inevitable to focus our attention to these factors in the sports preparation of children and youth.

In sports preparation, modelling is mostly used for the solution of the following tasks:
1. Prediction of the result of the particular training process, i.e. how the situation will be changed after the performance of the planned training.
2. Method of proceeding in the given situation so that we modify it in the desirable direction, i.e. to reach a change from starting situation to the terminal one.

In the sphere of top sport, coaches use models of the long-term sport preparation. In these models they aim to bring an athlete from the initial position into the terminal (desired) one. Models of long-term sport preparation are dynamic developing systems which apart from being informatory, also inspire meaning and provide a way to elaborate plans for the sports preparation of particular athletes, in particular kinds of

Table 1.1: Distribution of indicators of functional preparedness of an athlete as to their importance (Nabatnikovová, 1982)

Level of importance	Groups of sports				
	Explosive	Cyclic	Demanding a high degree of coordination	Martial arts	Sports games
I	1,2	1,5,7,8,9	1,2,3,6	1,2,3,6	1,2,3,4
II	6	2,3,6,10	4,5,7,8,9	5,7,8,9	5,6,7,8,9
III	5	4	10	4,10	10
IV	3,4				

Explanations: 1 – kinesthetic analyser, 2 – vestibular analyser, 3 – visual analyser, 4 – acoustic analyser, 5 – endocrine system, 6 – peripheral muscle-nerves system, 7 – cardio-vascular system, 8 – respiratory system, 9 – system of metabolism, 10 – thermal regulation system.

sports. Specific plans must respect age, sexual, and individual peculiarities, as well as social and material condition. The quality of the model always depends on the scope and level of knowledge used in the creation of the model.

In order to create a model of long-term sport preparation in volleyball, it is essential to devise the necessary fundaments, represented as follows:
1. The structure of sports performance in volleyball.
2. Age dynamism of the development of factors of the structure of sport performance, as well as intergender and individual peculiarities of the development of individual factors of the sports performance.
3. Dynamism of increasing training and competitive loads, as well as increasing sports performance.

Sport training is a process of complex biological, psychological, and social adaptation, in which an athlete is systematically loaded by a set of specific stimuli, in order to improve reactions, sport form, develop motor abilities, personal qualities, acquiring knowledge, motor skills, tactical acting, behaviour and to improve sport mastery.

Coordination can be defined as "cooperation of central nervous system and skeletal muscles within some aimed movement process" (Holmann & Hettinger, 1990). Quality of coordination depends principally on processes of movement control and the connected nervo-muscular processes, as well as on the level of analysers.

Movement coordination is defined as "temporal, spatial and power control of individual movements or complex motor expressions, which are executed with regard to tasks and goals handed over through senses" (Mechling, 1983).

Coordination abilities. Hirtz (1985) defines coordination abilities as "complex, relatively independent prerequisites of performance regulation of movements, which are created and developed in motor activities based on dominant, inherited but influenceable neuro-physiological functional mechanisms and therefore, they can be improved by means of a methodical training." Kirchem (1992) states that the terms "skill" and "agility" used before, are not able to explain the complexity of coordination abilities and to describe their structure. We deal with the problem of relationship between coordination abilities and motor skills (technique) in other chapter.

Reaction speed is an ability to react quickly by an adequate (standard or non-standard) movement activity on a certain stimulus (acoustic, optic, tactile, kinesthetic) or actual change of situation (Hirtz, 1985). Impulse can be also a moving object (ball, puck, team-mate, opponent). We differentiate between a simple and complex motor reaction. In sport games complex motor reaction (reaction with an option) is the most common requirement; this requires fast selection from various options of such motor reaction, depending on which is most adequate and effective for the given situation, and which would lead to success with the largest probability. Gamble (2013) states that perception-action coupling and decision-making are critical elements in terms of developing the ability to express reaction speed and agility capabilities under match conditions.

Kinesthetic-differentiation ability is an ability to control movements in time, space and dynamics, which allows for reaching a high precision and fine harmonizing of individual phases, as well as movement activities as a whole. It requires conscious and perfect harmonization of the movement with the motion conception. Among the specific expressions of this ability belong "sense of movement", "sense of a ball or a puck", "sense of tempo" (Hirtz, 1985).

Space–orientation ability is an ability to learn fast and adequately change the position and movements of the body in space in relation to the external environment (court lines, team-mates, opponent, ball, goal) (Hirtz, 1985). This enables the player to have accurate orientation in any game situation and coordinate movements in compliance with the real movement task. It depends to a great degree on the quality of vestibular apparatus.

Rhythmic ability is an ability to grasp and simulate temporal and dynamic segmentation of the course of movement (Hirtz, 1985). We speak mostly about accomodation of the movement to the given (external) rhythm or finding an optimum and effective internal rhythm, allowing for reaching higher effectiveness of motor activity. Related to this also is the ability to accomodate to the motor rhythm of other athletes, team, to change rhythm of playing, to enforce one´s own rhythm to the opponent.

Balance ability is an ability of an individual to maintain or restore balance of the body in situations where a fast or unexpected change in body position occur (Hirtz, 1985). Balance involves a host of sensorimotor capacities, comprising input from visual, vestibular and somatosensory systems (Bressel, Yonker, Kras, & Heath, 2007). It plays an important role especially in ice-hockey. It depends on the size of the weight-bearing surface, position of the body's centre of gravity, state of vestibular system and the CNS. Information from the vestibular systems is extremely important in terms of maintaining balance. We differentiate static and dynamic balance (from the point of view of sport games a high level of dynamic balance is required).

Besides the above mentioned 5 elementary coordination abilities there exist also other coordination abilities defined by various German authors:

Ability to redesign the motor programme. This ability allows for adjusting or rebuilding the original programme of operations during the performance (shooting at a goal, dribbling) based on perceived or expected changes to a situation, or to replace the motor programme by an adequate activity and to execute it (Schnabel & Thiess, 1993). Corrections can be carried out based on the change of situation and can be expected or unexpected, induced by the action of the opponent or team-mate (fighting for a rebound puck, getting loose from the opponent for a teammate). Changes of situation lead most frequently to the change of one parameter of movement. Ability to rebuild occurs, for example, in all operations and following interception actions between a defence and an offence players.

Ability to couple phases of movement. This ability ensures spatial, temporal and dynamic accuracy of movements of parts of the body within the movement of the whole body aimed at certain movement target while contacting a ball and the opponent (Schnabel & Thiess, 1993). It is manifested in an effective bonding of simple movement phases, or game activities into a complex sport activity, in partial movements executed either consecutively or simultaneously, uninterrupted but targeted, fluently and interconnectedly.

Agility. This term comprises the ability to stop, rapidly change direction, and accelerate in response to an external cue. Agility is required by many sports (Bloomfield, Polman, O´Donoghue & McNaughton, 2007; Gabbett, Kelly & Sheppard, 2008; Little & Williams, 2005). Some literature uses the term *quickness* synonymously with *agility* or *change-of-direction speed* (Moreno, 1995; Sheppard & Young, 2006). However, Sheppard and Young (2006) suggested that the definition of *quickness* does not consider deceleration or a change of direction and that quickness in and of itself contributes to agility. The literature indicates that agility must consider not only speed but also the ability to decelerate, change direction, and reaccelerate in response to stimuli. Agility is thus, a complex set of independent skills that converge for the athlete to respond to an external stimulus with a rapid deceleration, change of direction, and reacceleration (Sheppard & Young, 2006; Young, James, & Montgomery, 2002). These experts suggest that agility is affected by the athlete´s perceptual and decision-making ability and the ability to quickly change the direction.

Eye–hand coordination (also known as *hand–eye coordination*) is the coordinated control of eye movement with hand movement, and the processing of visual input to guide reaching and grasping along with the use of proprioception of the hands to guide the eyes. If you want to learn how to improve eye-hand coordination, you are tuning a fine motor skill that develops shortly after birth. It is an important task regardless of your age. Children are taught how to improve eye-hand coordination as early as 4 months old through exploring of toys and games. Practicing this skill not only helps with daily activities or with a specific athletic sport you are trying to improve upon but it can also help delay the aging process.

Vision is the process of understanding what is seen by the eyes. It involves more than simple visual acuity (ability to distinguish fine details). Vision also involves fixation and eye movement abilities, accommodation (focusing), convergence (eye aiming), binocularity (eye teaming), and the control of hand-eye coordination. Most hand movements require visual input to be carried out effectively. For example, when children are learning to draw, they follow the position of the hand holding the pencil visually as they make lines on the paper. Between four and 14 months of age, infants explore their world and develop hand-eye coordination, in conjunction with fine motor skills. Fine motor skills are involved in the control of small muscle movements, such as when an infant starts to use fingers with a purpose and in coordination with the eyes.

1.1 Modelling the Sport Preparation in Volleyball

Elaboration of the model of sport preparation is a difficult, complex task requiring thorough knowledge of the reality in this kind of sport, as well as honest preparation for its realization. Since motor activity in volleyball is of a non-standard character, it is very difficult to create a serious model of sport preparation. Long-term sport preparation through application of an optimum focus and content of preparation, should ensure a gradual development of all those factors of the structure of sport performance, which condition sport performance to a crucial degree.

From this point of view, it is inevitable to know all the factors which form the structure of sport performance in volleyball. Modelling the preparation in sport games requires applying optimum focus and content of preparation, procedure of reaching this target status, as well as information on desired changes of individual factors of performance in compliance with age-related developmental changes.

An important prerequisite of effectiveness of the model of coordination preparation is the prognosis and application of training loads, optimum in volume, intensity, coordination complexity and psychological demands, as well as a gradual and sufficiently progressive increase in individual stages of the long-term sport preparation.

To summarize, it is possible to say that among the crucial prerequisites for the elaboration of the model of coordination preparation in volleyball belong:
- The knowledge of limiting factors of the structure of sport performance;
- The knowledge of the growth of sport performance and the decisive factors of its structure in the course of the long-term sport preparation;

- The knowledge of dynamism of increase of load in the course of the long-term sport preparation.

1.2 Characteristics of the Sport Preparation in Sport Games

A constituent part of sport training in sport games is the fulfilment of various tasks which are called components of sport preparation. Only acquisition of all the components, which create the whole complex mosaic of the process that is called sport training, can lead to an optimum growth of performance level.

Individual components are represented in sport training in various ratios depending on the period in which the athlete is situated. When the sportsperson is in full preparation for competition or a tournament, the preparation contains predominantly technical and tactic means and in the period one or two months prior to the beginning of the competition period there prevails conditioning. However, it is important not to forget about maintaining a certain level of conditioning, as well as coordination abilities, even during the competitive period. This factor is frequently underestimated by coaches and also players, who refer mostly to fatigue and fear of overtraining. An important role is also played by the quality of recuperation processes.

At present, the classical division into preparatory, competitive and transition periods in certain sports is rather old-fashioned. It is due to the fact that in sport games like tennis (outdoor and indoor, winter and summer tournaments) or volleyball (competitions, tournaments, cups and national and international competitions, beach volleyball in summer) the competitive period lasts all the year round. Of course, we speak mainly about top-class or elite sport.

In the preparation of youth sport we can remain at "classical division", therefore, we consider it important to know the inherent laws of training periods and training components.

The preparatory period consists of two stages. The task of the preparatory period in the first stage (preparatory period 1) is to create functional prerequisites for further growth of performance. The basic task of preparation is to increase condition by means of overall and special conditioning. Training is mostly focused on the development of aerobic capacity of the organism. In this period, the means of overall and special physical preparation blend together in a certain ratio, see Table 1.2 which shows an outline representation of components of sport training in individual training periods.

Besides other components of sport preparation such as technical, tactical, theoretical, psychological preparation and medical observation, conditioning plays the most important role since it is the decisive determinant for all sport activities. The importance of conditioning is manifested in various age categories in different proportions. A core of conditioning is formed by the development of motor prerequisites

Table 1.2: Components and periods of sport training in the year cycle in % (Felix, 1997)

Components of sport training	Preparatory period I.	Preparatory period II.	Competitive period	Transition period
Overall conditioning	70	10	-	90
Special conditioning	20	50	10	-
Technical and tactical preparation	-	35	75	-
Psychological preparation	-	-	5	-
Theoretical preparation	5	5	5	-
Medical observation	5	-	5	10

of an athlete. Reaching the level of sport performance is a long-term and multifactorial process, in which the development of motor abilities has an inseparable part. This growth is carried out based on adaptation changes being in progress in the particular physiological, functional systems and corresponding psychological processes and is conducted in cooperaton with the acquisition of motor skills and habits.

In compliance with Šimonek and Zrubák (1995) we can define conditioning as "pedagogical process focused on increasing functional and psychic possibilities of an athlete, strengthening health, overall physical growth and creation of such motor potential of an athlete, which shall alow him to reach a high level of sport mastery upon applying rational technique and tactics and upon optimum utilization of personal prerequisites".

From this definition it appears necessary to also specify separately"coordination preparation" although this did not exist in the past. Based on research, coordination abilities and conditioning abilities form at least equivalent prerequisites in humans for optimum motor activity and thus we assume that our reqirement to introduce a new term "coordination preparation" is eligible.

Conditioning plays the most important role in the training of children and youth where it fulfills two functions:
1. Overall physical preparation, which is focused on the development of functional possibilities of an organism based on general motor development,
2. Special physical preparation, focused on maximum development of motor abilities, limiting sport performance in the given sport specialization.

Overall and special conditioning preparation form a unit and that is why also overall preparation must be related to the given sport branch. Correctly focused conditioning can result in an optimum state of physical and psychic preparedness of an athlete according to Dovalil et al. (2002). The importance of conditioning is manifested in specific proportions in various ages, in various sport branches and on different performance levels.

Youth training requires a specific and quite different approach to design and implementation of physical preparation. As famously stated by Tudor Bompa, young people cannot merely be considered "mini adults" (Bompa, 2000). The physiological makeup of children and adolescents is markedly different from that of mature adults (Naughton et al., 2000) – it follows that the parameters applied to training design should reflect these differences.

The young athlete´s neural, hormonal and cardiovascular systems develop with advances in biological age, leading to corresponding changes in neuromuscular and athletic performance (Quatman et al., 2006). Rates of development of a number of physiological and physical performance parameters measured in young team sports athletes are shown to peak at approximately the same time as they attain peak height velocity (Philippaerts et al., 2006). The age at which this occurs is highly individual; "typical" ages are around 11.5 years for females (Barber-Westin et al., 2006) and for males in the range of 13.8-14.2 years (Philippaerts et al., 2006). However, this can vary considerably – levels of biological and physiological maturation can be markedly different between young athletes of the same chronological age (Bompa, 2000; Kraemer & Fleck, 2005).

In early childhood there prevails overall sport preparation (development of an overall fitness), with an increasing age and growth of sports performance the ratio between overall and special physical preparation equalizes and in the stage of top training special physical preparation represents only a small share (Tab. 1.3).

The specified shares of components of sport training which generally apply may be modified in different sports depending on the periodisation of sport preparation.

In volleyball, coaches must often solve the problem of improving the quality of physical preparedness of a player, when increasing the volume and intensity of loading does not bring the required effect. From this point of view, several experts have shown through experiments that the development of strength, speed, endurance and flexibility is enhanced when preceded by good quality goal-oriented coordination development. This, in turn, forms a base for reaching the level of sport mastery in the shortest time.

The level of coordination abilities in volleyball underlies markedly the quality, tempo and stability of the acquired sports skills, as well as their perfect utilization in game activities. Since the components of coordination develop mostly in the period before puberty, it means that the crux of the development of coordination abilities falls into the period specified by the stage of elementary sport preparation.

From the point of view of periodization of sport preparation, the specialized coordination preparation plays the most important role in the second preparatory period, when the athlete prepares for acquisition of technically demanding motor skills.

Table 1.3: Ratio between generally developing and specialized exercises in the preparation of children and youth (Kampmiller, 1991)

Components of conditioning preparation	Age										
	9	10	11	12	13	14	15	16	17	18	19
General sport preparation	85	85	80	70	65	60	40	30	20	10	5
Special sport preparation	0	0	3	7	5	5	15	20	25	30	35

Explanatory notes: Data on overall and special preparation specify percentage, which belongs to conditioning besides other components of sport preparation of a young athlete.

The substance of the special physical preparation in sport games can be seen initially in the development of coordination abilities of a player, which then determine not only quality but also degree of utilization of conditional factors. Analysis of activity in sport games shows that many athletes have shortcomings in individual technical prerequisites. Particularly in the conditions of a game, the player is not often able to master the technique in an optimum way and to utilize the experience obtained during the training. One of the reasons for this can be an insufficiently developed coordination base of an athlete. These inadequacies can be removed if a goal-oriented and systematic programme of development of coordination abilities is conducted in parallel with the skills acquisition phase. Knowing the coordination prerequisites limiting the performance in sport games is essential in order to increase sport preparedness of a player.

2 Factors in the Structure of Performance in Sport Games

A rational model of coordination preparation essentially emerges from knowledge of the factors structuring performance in sport games. Sport performance forms a "complex system of factors, which are arranged in a certain way, there exist mutual relations among them and in their entirety they are manifested in the level of performance" (Dovalil et al., 2002).

Zaciorskij (1979) underlines the great importance of the knowledge of factors of the structure of sport performance while pointing to the need to solve the following problems:

1. Which factors underlie the performance in the given sport game.
2. What are the mutual relations among these factors.
3. What is the degree of importance of individual factors for the performance in the given sport game.
4. The knowledge of structure of sport performance in time, since in various age categories some factors are more important than others but after a time their importance can change. This means that the current level of preparedness and the state of the organism should be evaluated from the point of view of prospective requirements of the model structure of the sport performance. As a result of the structural requirements of the sport performance and the functional structure of the human organism there exist two integrated levels on which sport performance evolves.

When solving the given groups of problems we shall depend on the current knowledge of authors who have been dealing with these problems (Choutka & Dovalil, 1991; Dovalil et al., 2002; Mangi, Jokl, & Dayton, 1987; Nabatnikovová, 1982; Jonath & Krempel, 1991; Letzelter, 1978; Schnabel & Thiess, 1993; Schnabel, Harre, & Borde, 1994). All authors agree that sport performance is the result of a cooperation of many factors (Fig. 2.1).

In the structure of sport performance we can differentiate the following spheres:
- Genetic predispositions (physiological, psychological and somatic)
- Prerequisites of personality
- Motor predispositions (motor, conditioning potential)
- Coordination prerequisites and mastering the sport technique
- Sport tactics
- Social environment and conditions

Top sport, which is characterized by an effort to progressively increase sports performance, poses higher and higher claims on sports preparation, accruing from the necessity of permanent improvement of its contents. Sports performance, which

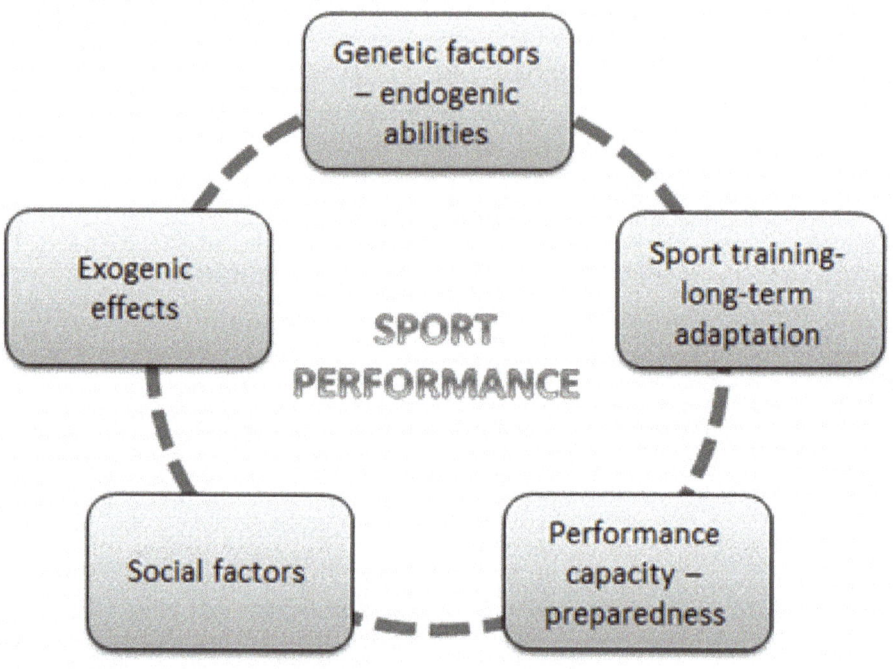

Fig. 2.1: Multifactorial character of sport performance (Felix, 1997)

is our main interest, is an "expression of materialized abilities of an athlete developed by the goal-oriented long-term sport training process" (Choutka & Dovalil, 1991, p.13). In order to understand the substance of game performance of a player we based our work on the following definition: "Human activity is the process controlled by the nerve system, in which we influence our living environment and stimulate changes in it which are focused on benefitting the individual, society or species".

Emerging from this it is possible to create a complex model of the game activity of an individual player represented proportionally through eight components:

1. Power components, i.e., high level of functional preparedness of an organism to bear training and game load.
2. Motoric component, i.e., the corresponding level of development of motor abilities and acquired motor skills.
3. Intellectual component, i.e., adequate level of knowledge, ability to think creatively and problem solve.
4. Motivation component, i.e., high level of performance motivation, cognitive needs and tendencies towards creative activity.

5. Will component, i.e., high psychological stability, ability to overcome unfavourable competitive states.
6. Social component, i.e., adequate level of social-interactive skills of cooperation and communication in a sport group.
7. Adaptation component, i.e., developed ability to self-control one´s own acts and behaviour, ability to adapt to the environment, to change it, to change oneself.
8. Integrating and controlling component, which coordinates and controls all others into an integrated act of the personality.

Sport games in modern understanding are highly dynamic and changeable phenomena and knowledge of their essence requires a deeper analysis and insight into their finest structure.

Nabatnikova (1982) recommends dividing structural factors of sport performance into three categories according to the importance:
- *First category*: factors which directly limit sports performance in a specific sport and might not be compensated for.
- *Second category*: factors which underlie sports performance in a specific sport, and can be at least partially compensated for.
- *Third category*: factors which directly do not underlie general sports performance but create necessary prerequisites for the development of factors of the first two categories.

Choutka and Dovalil (1991) present the following classification of sport performance, according to which the majority of sport games belong in the group of collective performances, which require a high level of control by the central nervous system as well as analysers (anticipation, decision under time pressure, sensomotoric coordination in time and space, claims for a static and dynamic balance, claims for variability and application of the trained potential in the constantly changing conditions of a sports match (Tab. 2.4)). Performance in sports games places a complex set of requirements on players. It consists of a large number of operations and acts, which are focused on realization of a certain aim, are logically structured as to time and controlled by voluntary processes. The majority of these game activities are realized in non-standard conditions, thus impeding the posibility of their acquisition and improvement in the training process.

Table 2.4: Characteristics of a motor activity in sport games (Choutka & Dovalil, 1991)

Type of sport performance	Sport event	Solved task	Characteristics of a motor activity		
			Motoric	Physiological	Psychological
Team sport	Voleyball Soccer Handball Basketball Ice-hockey Field-hockey Water-polo.	Overcoming active opponent by individual, group or collective means.	Number of movements or skills is large, complex movement structures, creative coordination, large variability.	Medium power uptake, regulation of motor activity on quality under the long-term load, cardio-vascular and respiratory systems are loaded medium to maximum.	Voluntary activity, controlled aggression, creative tactical thinking, decision under time pressure, anticipation, team thinking and acting, high motivation, high claims for coordination in time and space, earnest attention and fast reaction, claims for dynamic balance.

3 Coordination Abilities and Their Impact on Sport Performance

From the point of view of resolving our problem, we shall deal with the problem of coordination prerequisites as one of the limiting factors in the structure of performance in sport games. The impact of coordination abilities on sport performance changes depending on the specific requirements of the sport game. Similarly, from the point of view of the structure of individual coordination abilities various factors contribute to the final performance in a diferent way.

Differentiation of individual coordination abilities has a practical meaning also in talent selection for sport games, since each game is characterized by certain coordination abilities which create an important part of structure of the sport performance.

Coordination abilities share factors in common with the components limiting sport performance in sport games, however, their exact percentage cannot be unequivocally stipulated. It will depend on age, sex and amount of sport preparation in the period in which the sport performance is assessed. Different authors have attributed various values to coordination abilities (Tab. 3.5 and 3.6).

Tables 3.7 and 3.8 show motor abilities from the point of view of their importance for individual sport games, as seen by some international experts.

Based on the given complex model of game activity in sport games it is possible to state that in order to reach top mastery, completion / performance of all components of activity is inevitable. Current knowledge makes it very difficult to state the relative weighting of specific individual components of activity contributing to top performance

Table 3.5: Share of components of motor potential on the performance in sport games (Mangi, Jokl & Dayton, 1987)

Components	Ice-hockey	Basketball	Soccer	Tennis	Voleyball
Aerobic endurance	3	3	3	3	2
Speed abilities	3	3	3	3	3
Strength abilities	3	2	2	2	2
Anaerobic endurance	3	3	4	3	2
Flexibility	2	2	2	3	3
Coordination abilities	3	4	4	4	3

Explanations: Scale of points in assessment – 1 (min. value) through 4 (max. value).

© 2014 Jaromír Šimonek
This work is licensed under the Creative Commons Attribution-NonCommercial-NoDerivs 3.0 License.

Table 3.6: Share of components of motor potential – conditioning as well as coordination abilities – in several sport games (Jonath & Krempel, 1991)

Components	Soccer	Handball	Basketball	Volleyball	Tennis
Speed abilities	20	25	20	15	15
Strength abilities	15	20	25	45	15
Endurance abilities	30	15	30	10	25
Flexibility	15	15	10	15	10
General strength	-	10	-	-	-
Coordination abilities	20	15	15	15	35

Explanations: Numeral values represent percentage of share on the factor of fitness

Table 3.7: Rate of importance of motor abilities from the point of view of sport performance in sport games (Nabatnikova, 1982)

Rate of importance	Decisive motor abilities
Factors – Group I	4, 5, 10
Factors – Group II	1, 2, 3, 7
Factors – Group III	6, 8, 9

Explanations: 1 – speed abilities, 2 – speed-strength abilities, 3 – maximum power, 4 – explosiveness, 5 – relative power, 6 – power endurance, 7 – special endurance, 8 – aerobic endurance, 9 – flexibility, 10 – coordination abilities

of a player. We assume that coordination abilities form part of a minimum three components of the motor activity of a player (components no. 2, 7 and 8) and play a very important role in the overall sport performance in sport games. For this reason, we shall try to create an optimum, rational model of coordination preparation in sport games with the focus on volleyball.

This model of sport preparation is not a stereotype template but it should serve coaches as a base for elaboration of specific plans of sport preparation for individual sport games with the focus on the development of coordination abilities in individual stages and cycles of sport preparation.

Table 3.8: Influence of some sport games on the development of motor abilities of players (Derka, Gottschling & Kunz, 1995)

Motor abilities	Volleyball	Soccer	Basketball	Handball	Ice-hockey	Tennis
Speed	XXXXX	XXXX	XXXXX	XXXXX	XXXXX	XXX
Strength	XXX	XXX	XX	XXX	XXX	XXX
Endurance	X	XXX	XXX	XXX	XXXXX	XX
Coordination	XXXX	XXXX	XXXX	XXXX	XXXX	XXXXX
Flexibility	XX	XX	XX	XX	XX	XXX
Power endurance	XXX	XXX	XXX	XXXX	XXXX	XX

Explanations: Number of X explains size of effect on the development of motor abilities

3.1 Definition and Structure of Coordination Abilities

In the contemporary modern techno-society, as well as in top sport, importance of a person's prerequisites has increased, including abilities such as orientatation in space, differentiation of muscular perceptions and control of the rate of muscular extension, as well as speed of reaction to external environmental stimuli. Gross power is replaced by the development of manysided abilities – dynamic richness of motor coordination, motor intelligence, high stability and movability of functions of analysers.

Coordination abilities form an important role, which very often is a little appreciated part of motor prerequisites for motor activity. Měkota (2000), based on theoretical analysis of works of several authors (Schmid & Lee, 2011; Raczek & Mynarski, 1992; Waskiewicz, Juras & Raczek, 1999) determined the following model of hierarchical structure of the complexity of motor abilities (Fig. 3.2).

Factorial analysis considering 30 indicators of *coordination abilities* applied in a school population aged 7-18 years, which was executed by Raczek and Mynarski (1992) approved of five elementary, the so-called primary coordination abilities (I.). Each of the primary abilities, according to authors Waskiewicz, Juras and Raczek (1999), is then structured into sub-abilities (II.). Coordination abilities rarely exist in an isolated fashion and represent a mosaic of individual mutually interconnected abilities.

Generally, the term "coordination" can be defined as "cooperation of central nervous system and skeletal muscles within some aimed movement process" (Holmann & Hettinger, 1990). The quality of coordination depends principally on processes of movement control and the connected nervo-muscular processes, as well as on the level of analysers. The term "movement coordination" is accruing from the general definition

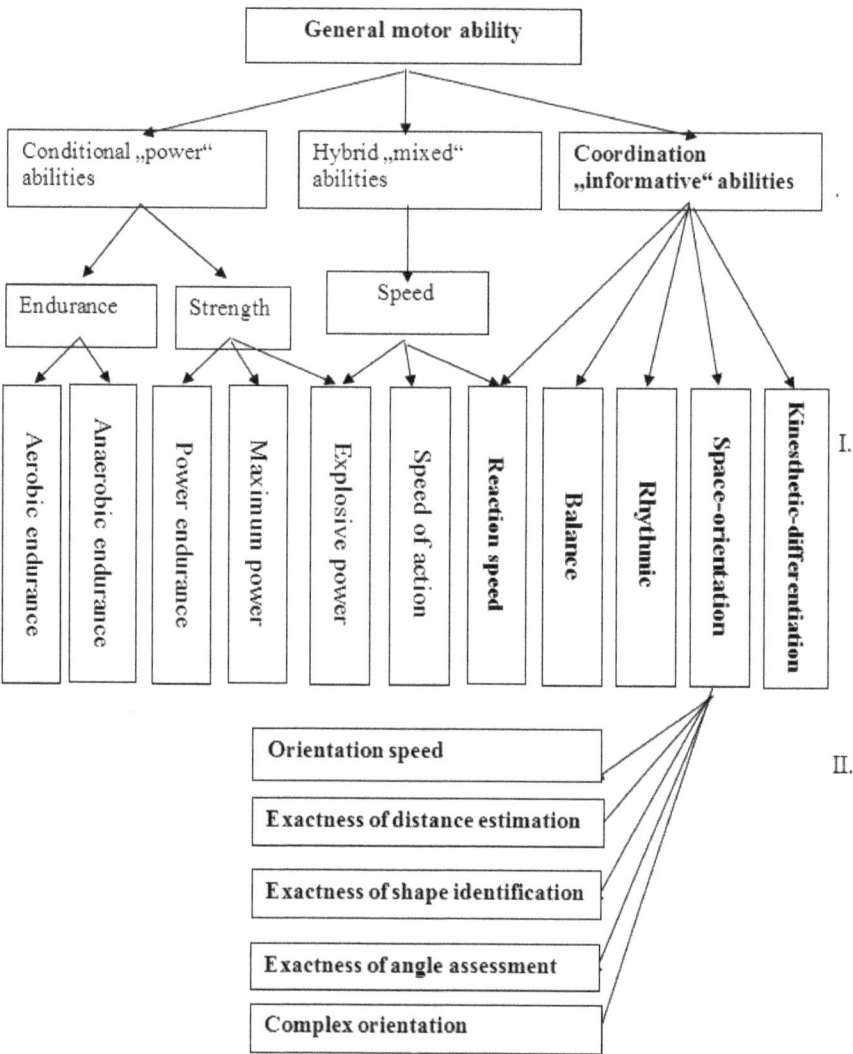

Fig. 3.2: Model of hierarchical structure of motor abilities by Měkota (2000)

of the term "coordination". This is defined as "temporal, spatial and power control of individual movements or complex motor expressions, which are executed with regard to tasks and goals handed over through senses" (Mechling, 1983). The term "movement coordination" should be understood as the superior concept, which encompasses the whole scale of coordination abilities. Kirchem (1992) states that the terms "skill" and "agility" used before, are not able to explain the complex of coordination abilities and to describe their structure. We deal with the problem of relationship between coordination abilities and motor skills (technique) in other chapter.

Hirtz (1985) defines coordination abilities as "complex, relatively independent prerequisites of performance regulation of movements, which are created and developed in motor activities based on dominant, inherited but influenceable neurophysiological functional mechanisms and therefore, they can be improved by means of a methodical training".

Coordination abilities are defined by Zimmermann (1983) as "relatively complex psychophysical traits, which co-influence sport performance. They create relatively lasting and more or less generalized qualities of the course of orientation and controlling processes, which control and direct sport activity". They are manifested in an "adequate updating of the programme of activities (regarding various conditions), in the tempo, kind and method of acquisition of new skills with regard to motor activities as well as in their applications of adequate situations but also in the degree of utilization and economy of condition potential" (Hirtz, 1985).

According to the authors Ljach, Mynarski and Raczek (1995), coordination abilities are not conditioned by somatic development and thus not by the somatotype. They have close bonds with psychophysical traits and are closely connected with conditioning factors, especially speed and speed-strength. The closest relationship is reported between coordination abilities and somatic development in girls aged 9-13 years and in 8-9 and 14-year-old boys. The least dependent are conditioning factors and somatic growth on the level of differentiation of dynamic, spatial and power parametres of movements.

Coordination abilities pose increased claims on the level of CNS and functions of analysers:

1. **Kinesthetic analyser** is a basic analyser for spatial, dynamic and temporal components of movement perception. It gives kinesthetic information on the processes of motor coordination and is important from the point of view of exact estimation of spatial, temporal and dynamic parameters of movement. The information comes internally rather than externally. Therefore, it is inevitable that the information received has been completed by other analysers.
2. **Tactile analyser** provides information on the shape and surface of objects, which are important for tactile activity. Also resistance of air or water are important information from the point of view of overall motor coordination.
3. **Vestibular analyser** provides information on the position of a head and on the direction and acceleration of the movement in relation to the head.
4. By means of an **optic analyser** we obtain information on one´s own movement acts and on the course of movment activities of other persons. Specifically in sports, where there is another moving subject – team-mate, opponent, goal, lines, ball, the movement of a player is controlled by visual information. Besides sharp sight, in several sports like basketball, ice-hockey peripheral sight is also applied, which is important from the point of view of correct motor coordination.
5. **Acoustic analyser** has an equal distance or telereceptoric character as the optical analyser. It offers relevant information for the motor coordination.

Coordination abilities are closely interconnected with the complex of conditioning abilities and form the least explored group of motor abilities. Opinions on their structure differ. Generally speaking "coordination" in the sense of motor coordination, can be understood as co-operation of the CNS and the skeletal muscles in the course of motor activity, while we differentiate:
a) intramuscular coordination (cooperation of tissues and nerves inside the muscle),
b) intermuscular coordination (inter-cooperation of various muscles).

In terms of connection with motor skills, Hirtz (1985) defines coordination prerequisites as "complex prerequisites for performance, which allow for learning and realization of motor skills and influence their expression".

Kasa and Šimonek (1999) define coordination abilities as "prerequisites of a man, serving for the synchronization of individual elements of movement into one whole upon solving the particular motor task. This integration is expressed in fair docility, ease and accuracy of movement, its timed realization. They condition speed and effectiveness of acquisition of inevitable motor habits, sport technique, thus facilitating reaching of high sport performances".

According to Měkota (1982), the high level of coordination abilities is manifested by the ability of a man to:
- coordinate individual partial movements (of body parts) – these are the so-called analytic coordination abilities,
- integrate movements into synchronized wholes – complex coordination ability,
- adapt, i.e. accomodate, adjust and modify motor activity according to the changing conditions – application of the complex coordination ability at adaptation.

Among other definitions by reputable authors can be mentioned the one by Schnabel, Harre and Borde (1994), according to which coordination abilities belong at the level of personal prerequisites for the performance related to the activity. The authors define coordination abilities as the "class of motor abilities, which are primarily conditioned by the processes of motor regulation and represent a relatively persistent and generalized developmental quality of these processes. They are the prerequisites for performance, which serve for the domination of the dominantly coordination claims".

To date, there is no generally accepted taxonomy of coordination abilities. In the past, this problem was addressed mostly from the neuro-physiological viewpoint (mechanisms of controlling and regulation of movements were accentuated). Today, pedagogical issues are the centre of attention allowing for the specification of individual coordination abilities.

Several experts (Hirtz, 1985; Ljach, 1988; Roth, 1982; Mynarski, Raczek, & Ljach, 1998) factorially analysed these movement prerequisites and found that coordination abilities have a relatively unified infrastructure for boys and girls aged 7-16 years. Rieder (1983) specified 53 various kinds of coordination abilities. Hirtz (1985) speaks about 80 different concepts. The majority of authors concur with the concept of Hirtz, who characterized 5 basic coordination abilities (kinesthetic-differentiation, space-orientation, rhythmic, reaction abilities and balance) with a suggested hierarchical arrangement into a system along with the abilities of motor learning, motor control and motor accomodation to changeable conditions.

Besides these five coordination abilities presented by Hirtz as basic ones, Schnabel (1994) complemented the structure with other two abilities – continuation of operations and transformation of movements. Hirtz (1985) defined individual coordination abilities as follows:

1. **Reaction speed** – ability to react quickly withan adequate (standard or non-standard) movement activity to a certain stimulus (acoustic, optic, tactile, kinesthetic) or actual change of situation (Hirtz, 1985). The impulse can also be a moving object (ball, team-mate, opponent). We differentiate between a simple and complex motor reaction. Sport games mostly entail complex motor reaction (reactions with options), which requires fast selection from a variety of options depending on which is most adequate and effective for the given situation, and would lead to the largest probability of success. As a rule these are non-standard operations which the player must synchronize with the operations of team-mates, opponents, the motion of a ball, and in relation to position on the pitch or court,as well as with respect to the rules of the game. In sport games, reaction speed limits directly the performance of a goalkeeper.
2. **Kinesthetic-differentiation ability** – ability to control movements in time, space and dynamics, which allows for reaching a high precision and fine harmonizing of individual phases as well as movement activities as a whole. It requires conscious and perfect harmonization of the movement with the motion conception. Among the specific expressions of this ability belong "sense of movement", "sense of a ball", "sense of tempo" (Hirtz, 1985). While a soccer player applies differentiation ability first of all at playing by leg or head, a basketball player, handball player, hockey player and volleyball player mostly does so through the movements of upper extremities. In sport games kinesthetic-differentiation ability allows for realizing an accurate pass to a certain distance (to execute a kick, throw or hit using a special dynamics), to perform a jump for a spike, heading in a correct time and on a correct spot, to carry out movements in a correct spatial and temporal flow.

A correct analysis of various conceptions of coordination abilities leads to their possible division into **general coordination abilities**, which are a prerequisite for any movement activity, and **special coordination abilities**, which decide on the quality of performance in individual kinds of sport activity and are specific for them. For example, in tennis the following specific abilities are the key ones: ball control, estimation of a distance and the so-called timing of the movement of a player with the flying ball, in compliance with the rules of the game; for ice-hockey it is a special dynamic balance while skating, the so-called "sense of a slide", then the ability of power slicing (kinesthetic-differentiation ability of upper extremities) while passing or shooting; there are also many other examples from different sport games. The concept of special coordination abilities emerges from the effort to derive concrete methodical and practical training instructions for sport practice, for which general coordination abilities are rather theoretical and abstract.

In relation to kinesthetic-differentiation abilities we have to mention the term **eye–hand coordination** which means the coordinated control of eye movement with hand movement, and the processing of visual input to guide reaching and grasping along with the use of proprioception of the hands to guide the eyes. If you don't have eye-hand coordination, you will see the ball but not hit it. It might hit your head if you are not careful!

If you want to learn how to improve eye-hand coordination, you are tuning a **fine motor skill** that develops shortly after birth. It is an important task regardless of your age. Children are taught how to improve eye-hand coordination as early as 4 months old through exploring of toys and games. Practicing this skill not only helps with daily activities or with a specific sport but it can also help delay the aging process (Bekkering & Sailer, 2002).

Vision is the process of understanding what is seen by the eyes. It involves more than simple visual acuity (ability to distinguish fine details). Vision also involves fixation and eye movement abilities, accommodation (focusing), convergence (eye aiming), binocularity (eye teaming), and the control of hand-eye coordination. Most hand movements (including volleyball skills) require visual input to be carried out effectively. Vision is developed in conjunction with fine motor skills between four and 14 months of age, when infants explore their world and develop hand-eye coordination Fine motor skills are involved in the control of small muscle movements, such as when an infant starts to use fingers with a purpose and in coordination with the eyes.

1. **Space–orientation ability** – ability to learn fast and adequately change the position and movements of the body in space in relation to the external environment (court lines, team-mates, opponent, ball, goal) (Hirtz, 1985). This allows the player to accurately orientate in any game situation and coordinate movements in compliance with the real movement task. It depends to a great degree on the quality of vestibular apparatus. Research show that implementation of exercises which load the vestibular system, in the preparation of volleball players, increased effectiveness of defence play and markedly decreased the percentage of errors upon net plays.

2. **Rhythmic ability** – ability to grasp and simulate temporal and dynamic segmentation of the course of movement (Hirtz, 1985). We speak mostly about accomodation of the movement to the given (external) rhythm or finding an optimum and effective internal rhythm, allowing for reaching higher effectiveness

of motor activity. Included in this also is the ability to accomodate to the motor rhythm of other players, team, to change the rhythm of playing, to enforce one´s own rhythm to the opponent. This ability plays a very important task for example in volleyball at effectively managing the run-up for spiking, or in basketball, at mastering the lay-up.

3. **Balance ability** – the ability of an individual to maintain or restore balance of the body in situations in response to fast and unexpected alterations in body position (Hirtz, 1985). It plays an important role especially in ice-hockey. It depends on the size of the weight bearing surface, position of the body'scentre of gravity, state of vestibular system and the CNS. For the keeping of balance information coming from the vestibular system have an extreme importance. We differentiate static and dynamic balance (a significant requirement in sport games).

4. **Ability to redesign the motor programme.** This ability allows for adjusting or rebuilding the original programme of operations during the performance (shooting at a goal, dribbling) based on perceived or expected changes to a situation, or to replace it by an adequate activity and to realize it (Schnabel & Thiess, 1993). Corrections can be carried out based on the change of situation and can be expected or unexpected, induced by the action of the opponent or team-mate (fighting for a rebound puck, getting loose from the opponent for a teammate). Changes of situation lead most frequently to the change of one parameter of movement. Ability to rebuild occurs, for example, in all operations and following interception actions between a defence and an offence players.

5. **Ability to bind phases of movement** – ensures spatial, temporal and dynamic accuracy of movments of parts of the body, within the movement of the whole body aimed at a certain movement goal while contacting a ball and the opponent (Schnabel & Thiess, 1993). It is manifested in an effective bonding of simple movement phases, or game activities into a complex sport activity, in partial movements executed either consecutively or simultaneously, uninterrupted but targeted, fluently and interconnectedly. This motor ability can be utilized in volleyball (run-up and spike), handball (ball dribbling – shooting), soccer and basketball (ball handling and shooting), tennis (return and approach to the net).

All individual coordination abilities are applied in motor activity of sport games in a complex, utilization of conditioned potential and the overall sport performance of a player depends on them.

In many sports games (Bloomfield, Polman, O´Donoghue & McNaughton, 2007; Gabbett, Kelly & Sheppard, 2008; Little & Williams, 2005), top athletes should acquire a high level of **agility**. Agility is thus a complex set of independent skills that converge for the athlete to respond to an external stimulus with a rapid deceleration, change of direction, and re-acceleration (Sheppard & Young, 2006; Young, James & Montgomery, 2002). These experts suggest that agility is affected by the athlete´s perceptual and decision-making ability and his ability to quickly change the direction. Some literature uses the term *quickness* synonymously with *agility* or *change-of-direction speed* (Moreno, 1995; Sheppard & Young, 2006). However, Sheppard and Young (2006) suggested that the definition of *quickness* does not consider deceleration or a change of direction and that quickness in and of itself contributes to agility. The literature indicates that agility must consider not only speed but also the ability to decelerate, change direction, and reaccelerate in response to stimuli.

Although it appears that perceptual decision-making factors can affect competition agility, there is a paucity of scientific data on this relationship. Šimonek (2013a; 2013b) published some results of the research into agility development in soccer, but this is just one of the multiple studies that should be carried out in order to specify the components of the complex ability in sport – agility.

3.2 Relationship Between Coordination Abilities and Motor Skills

In the sphere of technique (technical and tactical skills) exist rather deep reserves. Reaching the top level of sport mastery, i.e. successful utilization of technical means in a match, is a long-term and complicated process. Initial mastering of special motor skills as well as their improvement, acquisition of all special technical elements and their effective utilization in a match, requires a long-term training using various means and methods.

The process of training in sport games is particularly complicated. Besides such factors as conditioning and psychological maturity, technique, including coordination abilities, plays an important role. Blume and Hobusch (1982) differentiate two aspects of technique:
- motor skills,
- coordination abilities.

Improvement of motor skills belongs among the basic tasks of the year-long training process, in spite of the fact that it has not been solved at an optimum level. Several authors (Blume & Hobusch, 1982; Dobrý, 1982; Raczek, 1990; Kasa & Šimonek, 1991; Diaczuk, 1994) agree on the fact that there is a close relationship between coordination abilities and motor skills but that these should be differentiated. Měkota (1982) considers abilities as "more general, elementary, partially genetically conditioned internal prerequisites of a successful motor activity", while "skills represent dispositions acquired through learning and practicing based on the particular abilities".

The function of motor skills in physical education and sport is important from the point of view of those activities which are conditioned by coordination abilities. It is also when it is not effective that certain operations were automated, since they need a permanent change, accomodation and complexity. Motor skills are meaningful for those operations, which are of a creative character, such as activities of players in sport games.

Skills in sport games allow us to adequately adapt to the changing new conditions (change of the playing surface, colour and weight of the ball). Abilities express what level of motor performance can an athlete reach, how fast he or she can acquire the motor activity and how it will be improved. Abilities function and are expressed in a close connection with the acquired experiences in the performance sphere – skills.

Etzold (1973) attributed the concepts "gross and fine coordination" to the ones of "skill" and "technique". He assumes that "sport skill shows us to what degree the technique is acquired or mastered. The degree of "preparedness" of sport technique is realized in motor learning in three stages. Sport skill (and also technique) can be developed in three stages and is marked as gross, fine and extra fine coordination (variably dispositional)". Both skills acquisition and technique improvement underlie the laws of motor learning processes.

Rostock (1982) in his work on improvement of motor skills says that "First phase of motor learning results in gross coordination, which is gradually refined to a fine coordinated movement in the phase of strengthening and stabilization of the movement habit". Along with the improving quality of the course of movement the relationship between motor abilities and sport skills will become more and more close and thus also the qualitative level of both factors of performance – technique/coordination and condition(fitness), which is important mostly from the point of view of the development of coordination abilities in sport games.

Sport skills also relate to the acquisition and improvement of sport technique. Skills represent "readiness acquired through learning to solve correctly, quickly and economically a certain task, i.e. effectively execute a certain activity" (Choutka & Dovalil, 1991). If we consider that abilities are expressed through skills in motor performances, so the principle that abilities can be developed most favourably within the habits and skills, in which they are realized, must be truthful.

Insofar as it is not necessary to reach perfect and permanent acquisition of technique of motor activity, skills are only transitional stages of a motor habit. In sport games, where motor skills have a great meaning from the point of view of creative mastering of continuously changing game conditions, learning of movements is terminated by motor skills without the transition into the habits, as motor activity is conditioned by coordination abilities.

Raczek´s (1990) research provides evidence that the "level of coordination abilities is conditioned by the ability to learn new motor skills". In his experiments he found close relationships between the level of kinesthetic-differentiation ability and technique of the backhand stroke and between rhythmic ability and serve accuracy in tennis. Participants with a higher level of coordination abilities acquired new movement activities more quickly and accurately. Similar results were also found by Raczek in volleyball, where the closest relationships were found between the level of kinesthetic-differentiation ability and passing (setting), reaction speed, space-orientation abilities and defense play.

Current research studies focused on the structure of sport performance of a player are aimed at discovering the quantitative and qualitative characteristics of external manifestations of a player during a match; exploring the psychological processes of players; and attempting to empirically outline the structure of sport performance while specifying the relative contribution of individual factors creating it. According to Dobrý (1982) the complex available structure of a player´s performance is formed by:
1. senso-motor skills ensuring realization of a certain game activity,
2. coordination and speed motor abilities, conditioned by the level of movement control and forming an inseparable whole together with senso-motor skills,
3. motor abilities conditioned first of all by the level of particular energy-producing systems,
4. intellectual skills, conditioned first of all by the knowledge,
5. social-interactive skills flowing into effective activity of a player as a part of a sport team,
6. somatic characteristics,
7. psychological characteristics.

Understanding of the relationship between coordination abilities and motor skills allows us to disclose causes of a player´s failing, which are always manifested in an untrue and unsuitable form of motor expression. Dobrý (1982) can see the reasons for a player´s failing in connection with coordination abilities in:
1. insufficiently fine differentiation of individual partial movements,
2. unsuitable muscle relaxing,
3. inaccurate differentiation of power, temporal and spatial perceptions in the movement course of game activity of an individual,
4. change of the position and movement of the body within the area of the playing field at various temporal demands,
5. insufficient motor orientation in space connected with the perception of temporal parameters of movement and its changes,
6. organization of partial movements upon contacting ball and the opponent,
7. control of motor realization and its correction in conditions of an expected or unexpected change.

Relations between individual sensori-motor skills, relations between individual motor abilities and relations between sensori-motor skills and motor abilities, however, mostly coordination abilities can be considered as substantial parameters of sport performance of a player. We consider the relationship between sensori-motor skills and coordination abilities as the basic and necessary one. These relationships can be interpreted in the following way:
1. sensori-motor skills are manifested only by means of motor abilities,
2. motor abilities are manifested only by means of sensori-motor skills,

3. the level of coordination abilities determines the degree of utilization of conditioning potential,
4. stabilization of the player´s performance depends on the level of coordination abilities and their interconnection.

According to the research of Diaczuk (1994) the level of coordination abilities has an influence on technique in all stages of sport training, while the highest relationship was found between kinesthetic-differentiation ability and technique, as well as space-orientation ability, reaction speed and technique of junior handball players.

In sport practice we often meet the fact that players are well prepared as to conditioning; they can dash fast with the ball, can jump high, they are sufficiently powerful, but in spite of that the given conditioning prerequisites cannot successfully utilize and transform them into a high rate of success in a game. Results are then not economical in terms of their effort and time spent during sport preparation. There are topical questions to be answered such as: where to find the causes for the given failures and how to adjust and tailor the process of long-term preparation in sport games so that our athletes were also "sport virtuosos", "acrobats and jugglers" and "enchanters", who are able to amuse spectators. Answers to these questions are not so simple, however, we assume that our research suggests that if we shift the core of physical preparation more to coordination and technical side of conditioning and teach players motor skills under a certain "conditioning load" from the initial phases of sport preparation and not separately and without movement, they shall manage to control the ball at full speed, with mastery so that they are able to technically and physically overcome the opponent. Development of coordination abilities in compliance with the acquisition and improvement of motor skills and conditioning improvement will bring its "fruits" – goals and points and will contribute to the cultural experience of spectators.

3.3 Possibilities for the Development of Coordination Abilities

Coordination abilities show genetic determination and are relatively stable, internal prerequisites for the movement which can be developed by training. The largest increases can be recorded if we make use of the particular sensitive periods of their development. In these periods an increased sensitivity of the child to the influence of external stimuli is expected. The stimuli should be permanently created in order to facilitate the development of children. Hirtz (1985), based on his research of more than 1,300 participants, specified the following **sensitive periods for the development of individual coordination abilities:**

Kinesthetic-differentiation ability: 6-9 years
Rhythmic ability: 8-11 years
Reaction speed: 8-11 years
Balance ability: 8-12 years
Space-orientation ability: 9-14 years.

In the practice of sport games we often meet with several results of experimental observations of the development of coordination abilities in the school physical education and sport (Hirtz, 1985; Ljach, 1990; Šimonek, 1993, 1994, 1995, 1997, 1998; Šimonek et al., 2000) as well as in the sport training (Zimmermann & Nicklisch, 1981; Rostock, 1982; Zaťková, 1993; Diaczuk, 1994 – in handball; Schneider 1992; Melišová, 1996; Zháněl, 1999 – in tennis; Čechov, 1979; Brandt 1985; Raczek, 1990; Szczepanik, 1993 – in volleyball; Bora, 1996 – in track and field).
Results of experiments suggest that:
- coordination exercises positively effected the level of coordination abilities,
- tempo of motor learning in examined individuals has increased.

The level of technique and individual game performance has improved:
- in girls on average by 11% (passes: 16.2%, reception: 13%, spike: 9%); in boys on average by 16% (shot accuracy: 19.5%, pass accuracy: 13%).

Results of individual observation of girls suggest that the rapid somatic changes at the beginning of puberty have an effect on the level of coordination abilities (Fig. 3.3).

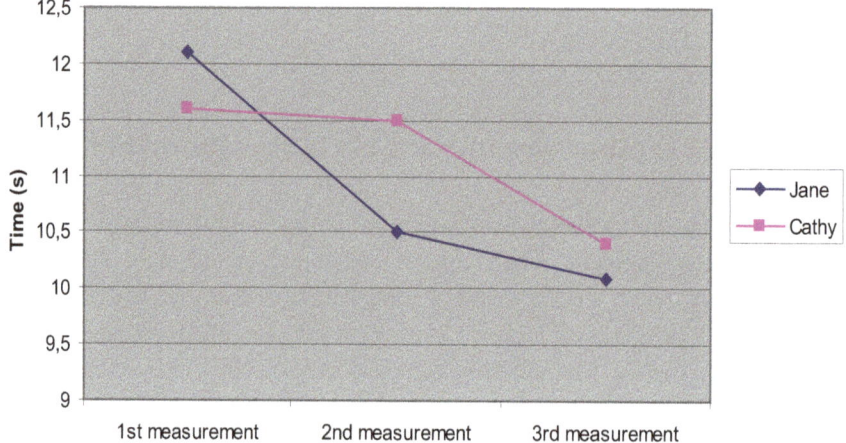

Fig. 3.3: Comparison of changes of the level of space-orientation ability in two girls (Jane and Cathy) of the experimental group (Šimonek, 1998)

For example, 12-year-old Cathy (in Slovak Katka) experienced a 9cm growth spurt during the last year, as a result of which the first period of specialized coordination preparation did not bring increases in the level of coordination abilities. Moreover, the growth spurt resulted in a lower level of motor skills. On the other hand, in the 11-year-old Jane (In Slovak Janka), who had not shown any signs of puberty beginning, had markedly improved in the coordination tests already in the first period.

It is evident that negative influences of biological factors (growth spurt, hormonal changes) should be compensated for by stressing social factors – in the form of supplementary sport activities or specially planned training, in compliance with the psychological requirements of an individual.

3.4 Methodology of Development of Coordination Abilities

The development of coordination abilities regarding future sport performance is aimed at acquisition of new, many-sided motor skills and their components. In order to reach this goal, various training methods and means are used in the training process. With regard to coordination abilities these can be devided into *general and special ones:*

General training methods and means serve for the improvement of the elementary level of coordination prerequisites. How much and with what effectiveness they can contribute to the improvement of the overall coordination, depends on the level of their development (Blume & Hobusch, 1982). The used training methods and means must correspond to the overall level of development of the athlete.

Special methods and means are directly connected with motor activities within sport competitions; their task is to improve sport specific coordination abilities (so-called sub-abilities) along with the cooperating analysers important for the given sport. Special training methods and means already require a high level of development of abilities and skills, and if they have to have the required effect, they should be acquired already in a more perfect and finer form (Weineck, 1980).

General and special methods are sometimes used in parallel in sport training. From the point of view of the required goal, coaches should know that the methods have special effects and should be applied accordingly. For successful acquisition of new sport skills principal importance is given to movement visualization, the creation of which precedes the process of learning itself. Depending on age, intellectual preparedness and obtained level of development of coordination abilities, two partial methods have been verified as crucial for the acquisition of a new movement visualization:
- *method of optical information*, which is specially suitable for beginning athletes,
- *method of verbal information*, which serves for the specification and clarification of the movement course. This method is used before, during and after the performance of the motor activity, while fulfilling the function of feedback.

3.4.1 Methods and Organization of the Development of Coordination Abilities

The following methodical principles of the development of coordination abilities can be recommended for the training practice:
- variation of the starting position (starting from various body positions like kneeling, laying on the back/front, sitting),
- variation of the course of performance of the movement (mirror exercises),
- variation of the movement dynamics (faster and slower movements in facilitated and hindered conditions, under a load, with a different weight),
- variation of spatial structure of the movement (decreasing the size of the field, obstacles of a different height and in different distances),
- variation of external conditions (playing on various surfaces, sand, clay, grass, changed dimensions of the field, playing in a windy and sunny conditions),
- variation of the information reception (hindered optical, tactile, acoustic or kinesthetic information (playing with dark goggles, with gloves, ball reception after the 180 degree turn, reception of a ball in volleyball with a masked net),
- combination of various game activities accompanied by an additional task,
- exercises under time pressure and under stressful conditions (balancing beam standing overhand passes – increased risk),
- gradual increase in complexity of exercises,
- newness, uncommonness, coordination difficulty of exercises,
- variegated repertory of exercises,
- smaller number of series and repetitions,
- sufficient interval of rest,
- implementation of coordination exercises into the preparatory part of the training session, after the warm-up, and also in the first part of the main part of the session.

Coordination abilities development methods:
- playlike and competitive,
- repetitive,
- variable exercises,
- under simulated conditions (anxiety, time deficit, fatique).

Forms of organization of exercises:
- frontal exercises and streamlike form,
- group exercises (in pairs, triplets, teams),
- exercises on posts (at least one or two posts should be devoted to the development of coordination abilities),
- supplementary exercises (increases the difficulty of performing the exercise as well as its effectiveness).

3.4.2 Methodical Hints for the Development of General and Special Coordination Abilities

From the point of view of long-term sport preparation, the aim is to create a base for complex motor activity athigher levels, i.e. accurate, errorlesss motor action. Key components of this process are coordination, condition, motivation, emotion, power, cognition. According to Kohoutek et al. (2005), relations between these components can be expressed as follows: high level of coordination towards condition inevitable for the sport technique with the utilization of control and motivating function of the intellect and stimulating-emotional effect. In the centre of the process of development of coordination abilities are motor skills. On the one hand, these are the goals of the training (didactic) process, and on the other, they serve as the means of development. The means can be divided into general and special ones.

General means of development of coordination abilities (Weineck, 1980):

1. *Movement and sport games* ensure complexity of the structure of conditions and allow for a controlled focusing on certain components of development (e.g. development of some analysers), thus avoiding certain special problematic situations (e.g., modified rules of the game). When acquiring new combinations and partial components of movement structures there comes to the synthesis of movement acts and their combinations, which, moreover, is done in difficult conditions (opponent, time stress, more difficult rules).
2. *Martial arts* develop not only condition but also coordination abilities, in mutual interactions such as opponents´ contacts. Factors such as reaction speed, decision making and problem solving are also important. There comes to the development of analysers, mostly kinesthetic, tactile and optic analysers are improving their function.
3. *Gymnastics and trampolining* allow for excellent proportioning of the degree of difficulty of partial components of the movement structures, or their combinations. Didactic training effect refers mainly to statokinetic (positional) analyser.

Special means for the development of coordination abilities have their foundations in the particular sport event. On the assumption that the movement requires high precision of control and we speak about fine movement correction or partial rebuilding of the movement structure, it is necessary to use such exercises, which shall satisfy just this requirement. It is important that coordination abilities and also analysers, which are responsible for the development of the overall coordination, specific for volleyball, were developed to the required level.

4 Age Dynamics and Intergender Differeces in the Level of Coordination Abilities

In sport games, and particularly in volleyball, the importance of technical and coordination performance factors has recently increased, since their level significantly influence the tempo, quality and stability of the acquisition of sport skills. In this way they facilitate the course of movement in the improvement and stabilization phases, determine the degree of utilization of the conditioned potential and allow for flexible adaptation of the movement to constantly varying conditions.

Based on several research works of mostly German sport scientists we can accept the fact that development of coordination abilities has a different course than that of the conditioning performance potentials (Hirtz, 1985; Juřinová, 1982; Ljach, 1988; Hartmann, 1992; Šimonek, 1993, 1998; Šimonek, et al., 1997, 1999; and others). Even if these authors applied various research methods, they basically agree that the most optimum interval for the development of coordination abilities can be considered between 7 and 12 years. This is the period of an intensive development of motor centres in the brain. At the age of 8, the development of the brain and head of children is already 90-95% of the maximum value (Weineck, 1996). "Fair reaction speed, courage, favourable somatic prerequisites, sufficient level of inevitable motor abilities, as well as high level of excitability and plasticity of the nerve system create favourable conditions for acquisition of the most difficult coordination movements" (Winter, 1975), (Fig. 4.4).

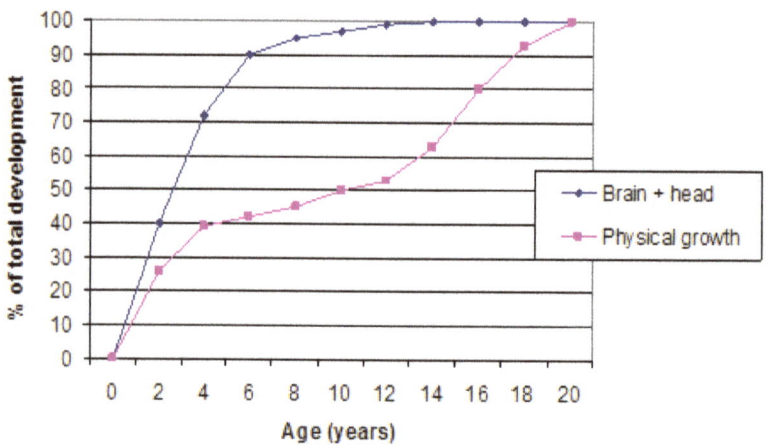

Fig. 4.4: Development of brain, head and overall somatic growth until adulthood (Weineck, 1996)
Explanations: Blue line = development of brain and head, red line = overall somatic development

© 2014 Jaromír Šimonek
This work is licensed under the Creative Commons Attribution-NonCommercial-NoDerivs 3.0 License.

Based on the research results as well as practical experience we can assume that between the ages of 7-12 years children can perform almost all movements (even the most complex), unless an extreme range of movements, considerable power, speed or endurance are required. That is why we can start teaching them even very difficult, complex motor skills (technique), which occur in sport games for example, lay-up in basketball, jump-up and spike in volleyball, timed pass in ice-hockey or soccer.

Israel (1977) emphasised the necessity to start methodical development during the pre-school years. Children upon entering school are able to successfully rate their efforts, to conform them to a certain rhythm, to slow them down.

The most intense phase of development is during the ages of 7-10 years while the overall development is almost finished in the first half of the school age. After the age of 12, there follows an interval of slower developmental dynamism and partial stagnation. This is conditioned both biologically and socially. In the initial school ages, in spite of the fact that a child shifts from the period of "free spontaneous movement" into the one of calmer, sedentary way of life, the child is developing under progressive conditions and age-specific changes in relation to the nervous system. Morphological development of the nervous system is almost completely closed until sexual adulthood. The kinesthetic-motoric analyser matures very early.

"Differentiation of spatial parameters, perception of time, maximum movement frequency of legs and fine motoricity of hands reach almost 75% of the overall increase for the whole school period already between 10th and 11th years of age. There comes also to a clear developmental shift in simple motor reaction to optical and acoustic signals similarly as upon distributing the attention. At the ages of compulsory school attendance there comes to an even development in space orientation ability, optical – spatial perception, differentiation of temporal parameters (about 75% of the total increase)" (Hirtz, 1985).

P.E. at school offers only a limited motor activity of children and youth, which causes delayed development in the growth of coordination abilities. Further development of substantially matured function of movement control is possible only through intensive stimulation of motor activity in children and youth.

Another reason can be low coordination demands in the pre-school age and younger school age (Frömel, 1982). Research by Zimmermann and Nicklisch (1981); Hirtz (1985); Brandt (1985); Raczek (1990); Szczepanik and Szopa (1993); Zaťková (1993); Šimonek (1994) and others suggest that by means of a long-term, systematic development of coordination abilities it is possible to reach positive changes in both sexes (by up to 15-20% for 12 months). It has been found that children involved in spontaneous sport activity in their spare time, do not experience stagnation of coordination development after their 12th year.

Problems of intergender differences in the level of coordination abilities have not yet been completely solved. Results of partial research are often contradictory and depend on the methodolgy used. Some authors (Raczek & Mynarski, 1992) think there is a differentiated development between boys and girls only after the commencement of puberty, while boys and girls by turns gain superiority in the quality of individual coordination abilities. Other authors (Hirtz, 1985; Ljach, 1990) suggest that although psychophysical functions show only minimal differences, in coordination abilities these were typical mainly after the age of 14. While it is possible to assume that the coordination maturity in girls occurs approx. 1 – 1.5 years earlier than in boys, the phases of stagnation are even more expressly marked.

Górska and Gierat (1995) concluded that no statistical differences in the level of coordination abilities were found in 13 year olds. Girls reached similar results as boys in the development of psychological – regulatory-controlling – processes, which determine the level of coordination abilities.

Šimonek et al. (2000) have not found (with some individual exceptions) statistically significant intergender differences between 6 – 22 year-olds coming from the regions of Nitra, Brno and Szeged (Figures 1-7, 22-25 enclosed). These researchers also found intergender differences only in space-orientation abilities, which suggests that brain structure differs in both sexes which is then manifested in functional differences relating to spatial visualization, perception of spatial parameters of movement and their changes. Males seem better equipped at solving spatial tasks while females fare better in precisely executing any motor tasks.

According to Kasa and Šimonek (1999) both men and women are similar in terms of coordination abilities which is why it is suggested that the development of coordination abilities during initital stages of sport prepartion in boys and girls should not substantially differ.

Lifelong courses of change the level of coordination abilities have an individual character in each individual. This is supported by longitudinal research carried out by Starosta and Hirtz (1985), who included in experimental group all children, not only those motorically talented. The authors discovered that a girl who grew 18cm over 2 consecutive years showed decreased levels of coordination abilities (a drop of 17 points) which consequently negatively influenced the process of acquisition of acquiring technique in sport training. Conversely, a girl who acquired early development of coordination abilities, showed that the growth spurt did not effect skill acquisition for a long time, and the level of coordination abilities started to increase again after a short period of stagnation. These experiences suggest that at an early development of coordination abilities and individual differentiation of requirements we can reach positive improvement of quality of the sport preparation of children and youth.

4.1 Peculiarities in the Development of Coordination Abilities at Ages 6-9 Years

The age of 6-9 years is an especially favourable period in the development of coordination abilities (Graphs 22 – 25). Girls during this age increase 28.6 – 92.3%

(on average 62.3%) and boys 22.5 – 80.0% (on average 56.2%) in indicators of coordination abilities (Ljach, 1989). That means that it is easily possible to achieve the development of these abilities in younger school ages, when there is an accelerated improvement of individual coordination abilities. If we neglect this period of accentuated external effect, we cannot expect a larger developmental effect in the following age category.

From the point of view of sequentiality influencing individual coordination abilities we can determine according to Hirtz (1985) the following order of influencing coordination abilities: at the age of 7-9 years-mainly kinesthetic-differentiation and reaction speed; at the age of 9–11 years – reaction and rhythmic abilities; and at the end of this period-balance (especially dynamic balance). During the ages of 7-11 years there is a substantial increase in fine motor skill, accuracy and rhythmic perception based on the high tempo of motor learning.

Based on our own research with children aged 5-6 through 10 years we recommend to develop coordination abilities in the pre-school age, as well as in the younger school age with an increased stress on the development of courage through increasing the risk-taking in a given motor task, and increased changing of conditions of exercises and motor rhythm.

It is necessary that teachers and trainers already in creches and primary schools regularly monitor the level of coordination abilities of children and assess changes over time. Knowing the tempo of motor learning as well as the level of motor abilities will enable teachers to suitably select and dose exercises and games with the aim of improving motor skills in children.

Through accented and variable training it is possible to reach remarkable changes in the course of development of coordination prerequisites for sport performance. This has been highlighted by several longitudinal experiments (Hirtz, 1985), cross-sectional studies (Ljach, 1989; Belej, Starosta, & Bajdziňski et al., 1994; Šimonek, 1997, 1999, and others), and also pedagogical experiments (Raczek, 1990; Zaťková, 1993; Szczepanik, 1993; Šimonek, 1994). At the end of the experiment, 11 year old children reached the performance of 15–16-year-olds. Particularly large increases were recorded in reaction speed, balance and kinesthetic-differentiation ability, while in the case of movements requiring fast acceleration and agility, the results were observed only after the first or even second years of experimentation. Rhythmic ability is improved depending on the age along with the maturing of the nervous system in children. No statistically significant inter-gender differences were found between boys and girls (Šimonek, 1999).

School sport has a positive influence on gross differentiation of muscular effort, fine proprioceptive perceptions should be developed by means of special means. Special groups of selected athletes show better ability of rhythmic perception and rhythmic performance on average than the common population. For example, tennis players and basketball players react better to acoustic stimuli. Young athletes, who train at least 4 times a week, show much higher indicators of this ability.

Table 4.9a: Percentage of individual performances of boys in the test "distance estimation"

Age	% share 1st attempt		% share 2nd atempt	
6-year-old	12.5	6.2	12.5	6.3
	40	41.3	33.7	47.5
7-year-old	25	10	15	10
	35	30	30	45
8-year-old	16.7	27.8	19.4	14
	19.4	36.1	33.3	33.3
9-ear-old	3.3	6.7	3.3	16.7
	23.3	66.7	35	45
10-year-old	6.7	6.7	6.7	16.7
	43.3	43.3	23.3	53.3

Explanations: Children had to drop a small cube as close to the centre of a square on the floor as possible. We divided the square into 4 smaller squares. Each square was marked with two symbols. Symbol (-) in the first position meant that the child placed the cube to the left from the centre, while symbol (+) in the first position meant that the cube was placed to the right. When symbol (-) was used in the second position it meant that the cube was placed nearer from the start position than the centre of the cube, while symbol (+) in the second position meant that the cube was placed too far (behind the centre).

When observing the level of distance estimation and motor memory we found out that with the growing number of attempts the inaccuracy of performing the motor task increased. We carried out testing, where children were asked to drop a small cube to the centre of a square (1m x 1m) at the distance of 10 m. They performed the task with their eyes closed. Based on the visual control after each attempt the movement performance was adjusted. In both sexes the ability to estimate the distance (in both protocols – with and without executing a 360° degree turn) is improving with the growing age. It is a paradox that in the test of distance estimation (protocol with a turn) the tested persons reached mostly better results than in the test protocol without a turn. We assume that under the influence of motor experience reached through individual attempts there comes to the improvement of motor realization of the set task, in spite of impairing the orientation by performing the turn (360 degrees) (Tab.4.9a, 4.9b).

Table 4.9b: Percentage of individual performances of girls in the test "distance estimation"

Age	% share	1st attempt		% share 2nd atempt	
6-year-old	40	6.5		31.2	3.2
	17.5	36		36.2	29.4
7-year-old	4.5	4.5		44.5	9
	54.5	36.5		36.5	50
8-year-old	6.3	15.6		28.1	12.5
	37.5	40.6		40.6	18.8
9-ear-old	5.9	11.8		11.7	17.7
	35.3	47		29.4	41.2
10-year-old	5.5	5.5		8.3	5.5
	50	39		33.4	52.8

Gerhát, Kollárovits and Teplická (1995) found the largest influence of motor learning on perception and differentiation of the spatial parameter. Ability to differentiate space was approximately identical in both sexes and the largest intra-individual differences were recorded only in the pre-school age, when probably the development of functional prerequisites of the organism of children had been concluded. Kollárovits and Gerhát (1993) propose that due to the unreliability of participants' performances in various age categories the level of certain coordination abilities is unstable.

Šimonek et al. (1999) observed a tendency to deviate when bringing an object to a target visual control is control is deprived after prior accurate distance estimations. The authors found out that 75% of participants brought the object shorter and more to the right (values minus-minus and plus-minus), which can be attributed to the influence of fear and uncertainty while performing the task. The deviation to the right side may result from the stronger right leg in right-legged pupils, who form the majority of the population.

4.2 Peculiarities in the Development of Coordination Abilities at the Age of 10-17 Years

The age period between 10 and 17 years (period of middle and older school ages) can be devided into three shorter periods which differ depending on gender (Graphs 22-25). At the beginning of this period there is no natural growth in the level of coordination abilities. However, in girls approximately at the age of 11-12 years puberty starts, which is marked by the negative influence of morphological indicators on the level of coordination. (See enclosed graphs). Puberty disturbs mostly balance and kinesthetic – differentiation abilities.

Boys enter puberty by 1-1.5 years later, thus prolonging the period of coordination disruption until the age of 14-16 years (Riegrová & Ulbrichová, 1998). After this period, in boys and girls we can record favourable increases in the level of certain coordination abilities, mostly space-orientation ability, balance and reaction speed (Šimonek et al., 1997; Hirtz, 1985).

Age dynamics of coordination abilities in the interval between 10–17 years has similar characteristics both in boys and girls and records an increasing trend with the exception of rhythmic ability (boys) and kinesthetic-differentiation ability of arms (boys – decrease, girls-stagnation). Stagnation and decreasing level of rhythmic ability in boys can be explained by the fact that boys generally do not engage in rhythmical exercises (rope skipping and the like) by the second grade of elementary school while girls continue in intentional development of rhythmic ability within the lessons focused on rhythmic and aerobic gymnastics. This depends on specific countries curriculum policy.

Worsened performance in boys when compared with girls in the test of kinesthetic-differentiation ability of arms ("Sitting target throw") can be caused by the growth in power in boys after the age of 11, which, however, misrepresents the performance in the precision throw (Šimonek et al., 1997).

Regarding complexity of the structure of coordination abilities and difficulty of their diagnosing, it is not so easy to characterize their developmental curves. Results in tests do not depend only on the level of the particular coordination ability but also on other motor abilities, which impact the resulting performance (e.g. performance in the test of space-orientation (Hirtz, 1985) does not depend only on the space-orientation factor but also other factors like reaction speed, acceleration speed, etc.). It is difficult then to determine to what degree the result in the test reflects the level of the coordination ability we intend to measure, and to what degree the level of other participating motor abilities.

Factors participating in the resulting performance are represented by a different measure which depends also on sensitive periods of their development. Space-orientation ability tested by a "Shuttle run" is an example. The level of this ability is increased in the pre-school age and in puberty. Girls reach their maximum at the age of 13 and boys at the age of 17. Then follows a gradual regression. Intergender differences occur only in the period of late puberty.

Movement accuracy depends mainly on the level of proprioception and the structure of joints. The largest increase in the level of this ability is reached by children aged 7-8 years. Another improvement comes between the 10th and 13th year and according to authors Riegerová and Ulbrychová (1998) it is related to the period of growth acceleration. Movement accuracy in upper extremities tested by a "Target throw" increases during childhood and adolescence, while the first peak in girls is reached at the age of 17 and in boys even much later. Regression in boys is even much more intense than in girls.

Static balance depends on the nervous system, particularly the vestibular system. The highest level is reached after year 17, at first in women and later in men. A massive growth in this coordination ability is between years 11 and 12 and later in boys after the age of 14, in girls a year later. Between years 11 and 13 in boys and 12 and 15 in girls there comes to stagnation and even decrease. Static balance in the pre-school age is better in girls, however, later boys take the lead.

Results of observation of dynamic balance show that this motor ability is provided by the level of nervo-muscular coordination and development of the nervous system (vestibular system). Large increase in the level of dynamic balance are recorded in the pre-school age, whereas during puberty we witness large oscillations with a marked regression in girls between the age of 12 and 14, in boys between 14 and 16. These intense oscillations are probably connected with the changes of the overall proportionality and growth acceleration, which are the causes of the change of the position of body centre of gravity along with the disruption in static balance.

Generally speaking, the most favourable periods are in first five years of school attendance and then after the end of puberty. Children obtain rudiments of motor coordination in the first grade of elementary school, on which they can build-up their sport mastery during their motor improvement programmes. However, one should not forget about the parallel improvement of coordination abilities and acquisition of motor skills, mainly later in the middle school age period.

Based on his research Hirtz (1985) specified that kinesthetic differentiation (function of motor analysers) develops first, a bit later reaction speed and relatively late the ability of space orientation (especially functions of static-dynamic and optic analysers). The development partially shows insignificant intergender differences: boys at first lag behind and later, as a result of being involved in sports, they develop their coordination abilities after the age of 13, which can be attributed also to the development of speed and speed-strength abilities at the sensitive period of 12-14 years. These facts suggest that coordination maturity precedes the sexual one.

One of the very few intergender differences, which coaches should take into consideration while planning the conditioning-coordination preparation, is the fact that coordination development is shifted forward by 1 to 1.5 years in girls and therefore the most suitable periods for the development of coordination abilities will also be prolonged.

4.3 Age Peculiarities in the Development of Coordination Abilities at the Age of 18-22 Years

No researchers have observed the level of coordination abilities in the age category of 18 and over so far. According to our research (Šimonek et al., 2000) we can list at least some preliminary facts (Graphs 22 – 25):
1. After the age of 18, coordination abilities are stable with only minimal deviations, in dynamic balance where development continues until a peak at the age of 22 years (Riegerová & Ulbrichová, 1998) and in space-orientation which shows a decrease.
2. After a transitory decrease in the level of coordination abilities at the beginning of puberty and a consecutive second favourable period (showing a positive influence), there are no marked shifts forward in the level of these motor prerequisites.
3. We have not found any significant gender differences in levels of individual coordination abilities in this age.
4. Even in the the period of junior and adult ages it is possible to reach certain positive changes in the level of coordination abilities, however, it requires a focused and long-term effort with specific focus of the sport preparation, especially in the preparatory and competitive periods.

5 System of Complex Control of the Level of Coordination Abilities

Many countries, including Germany, Russia, Poland, Czech Republic, USA and Japan have a rich experience in testing the motor performance of youth. The majority of research (Trzesniowski & Pilicz, 1989; Strel, 1990; Przeweda & Trzesniowski, 1992), however, concentrated on testing conditioning factors, while the level of coordination abilities is monitored only as part of the set (battery) of tests of conditional abilities, moreover, the sets mostly comprise only a single coordination test (overall or static balance test).

Works by Slovak and Czech researchers (Moravec, 1990; Moravec, Kampmiller & Sedláček et al., 1996, and others) have brought interesting knowledge on motor performance of the school population, however, in the latest motor test battery used in Slovakia – EUROFIT – we can find only a single coordination test - "Flamengo test".

In spite of the fact that much information on coordination abilities has emerged recently, only a few have been devoted to the monitoring of these prerequisites for movement (Ljach, 1989; Belej & Starosta, 1992; Kirchem, 1992; Belej et al., 1994) in children and youth between 10 and 17 years of age.

In Germany a group of experts on coordination under the leadership of Prof. Peter Hirtz elaborated test norms based on the measurement of over 1,300 children and youth and worked out age curves of coordination abilities.

It was discovered that when acquiring new sport skills (gymnastic, athletic, game-like) experimental group of pupils aged 4 to 6 achieved on average better results than older children of control groups.

In Russia Ljach (1989) presents a complex methodology of assessment and development of coordination abilities in his book "Koordynacionnyje sposobnosti školnikov" (Coordination Abilities of School Children). Norms were presented in the article "Testy i normativy urovnej razvitija koordynacijonnych sposobnostej školnikov" (Tests and Standards of Development of Coordination Abilities in School Children) (1988). In Russia the terms "lovkosť" (skillfullness) or "koordynacijonnyje sposobnosti" (coordination abilities) have been used.

In Poland the problem of testing was discussed by several authors (Trzesniowski & Pilicz, 1989; Žak, 1991; Przeweda & Trzesniowski, 1992; Raczek & Mynarski, 1992; Szczepanik, 1993). They use the terms "koordynacja ruchowa" (motor coordination) and "koordynacyjne zdolnosci" (coordination abilities).

Results of international research were presented by Belej and Starosta (1992). They elaborated standards for 11 to 14-year-old children, while they used two analytical and synthetic coordination tests. In Czech Republic we can mention authors Blahuš and Měkota (1983), who in their book "Motorické testy v tělesné výchově" (Motor Tests in Physical Education) present several coordination tests. Norms of coordination abilities were presented also by the authors Kohoutek et al. (2005).

© 2014 Jaromír Šimonek
This work is licensed under the Creative Commons Attribution-NonCommercial-NoDerivs 3.0 License.

In English written sources we can find only minor mentions on coordination abilities, which are denoted by the concepts "motor coordination", "coordination skills", "coordinative capacities" or "factors of coordination".

In Slovakia, the theory of coordination abilities has been developed by Kasa and Šimonek (1999), Šimonek, (1993, 1995), Belej and Starosta (1994), and others. In Central and Eastern European countries (Germany, Eastern Russia, Slovakia, Poland, Czech Republic, Hungary, Romania) the term "koordinačné schopnosti" (coordination abilities) is most frequently used, which replaced the older concept of "obratnostné schopnosti" (dexterities or skills).

In literature we can find a large number of coordination factors, but for didactic purposes there is a need to reduce their number. We will rely on the **7 elementary coordination abilities** identified by Blume and Hobusch (1982) especially when describing the structure of sport performance. The seven abilities comprise:

1. Kineshetic-differentiation ability
2. Space-orientation ability
3. Rhythmic ability
4. Reaction speed
5. Balance ability
6. Ability to rebuild movement programmes
7. Ability to bind movement activities.

5.1 Assessment of the Level of Coordination Abilities by Means of Performance Standards

In school, physical education and sport standards have been used as the main tool of assessment. Under a *"performance standard"* we understand such requirements on the level of motor abilities of pupils, which are expressed in an operationalized form, i.e. they are concrete activities, which the pupils must know how to perform in order to reach the goal of learning. Performance standard is considered to be a performance norm for pupils they have to reach and is strictly defined.

For a coach it is not difficult to define performance standards in the sphere of conditioning motor prerequisites, for example, a 10-year-old boy should reach the result of at least 160 cm to pass in the Standing broad jump test, however, it is more difficult to specify coordination standards. How can we specify the measure – norm of expected minimum performance (i.e. the limit of passing or failing the standard) for example in rhythmic coordination ability?

When preparing performance standards of coordination abilities it is necessary to pay attention to the fact that coordination abilities have a complex character and they should be assessed in a complex way, i.e. in one whole.

Based on a survey we elaborated performance standards for elementary coordination abilities (Šimonek, 1998) (Tab.1-14, Graphs 8-21 enclosed). For this purpose we set up a battery of 7 tests of coordination abilities, which includes the following rudimentary abilities: balance, rhythmic, reaction, space-orientation, kinesthetic-differentiation ability of legs and arms, ability to differentiate temporal parameters).

When assessing the level of coordination abilities we came out of the sum of assessment of individual coordination abilities, thus obtaining the complex picture of their level in individual age categories.

Performance standards of coordination abilities are evaluated in three levels so that an avarage and standard deviation are calculated and than, 3 performance standards are calculated for each age and gender category, separately for all 7 tests.

Performance standards in individual tests represent:
1. *Minimum standard* (MS = arithmetic mean + 1.75 s)
   Minimum standard upon coordination abilities stipulates minimum level of these abilities, which the individual should acquire in order to realize elementary skills, he is acquiring in volleyball.
2. *Optimum standard* (OS = arithmetic mean − 0.75 s)
   Optimum standard upon coordination abilities says that the individual has an optimum coordination prerequisites for the acquisition of motor activity, which forms a contents of sport preparation in the training process.
3. *Performance standard* (PS = arithmetic mean − 1.75 s)
   Fulfilment of the performance standard signalizes to the coach that the individual reaches a high level of coordination abilities, which predestines him for top sport performances and is a prerequisite for fast and perfect mastering of even difficult coordination sport skills. Performance standards, which we submit herewith, in charts and graphs, are not statistic norms but logical limits characterizing minimum, optimum or special level of coordination abilities.

5.1.1 Tests of Coordination Abilities

Based on the recent experiments (Šimonek et al., 1994, Šimonek, 1997, 1998) as well as the experience of other authors (Hirtz, 1981) we can recommend the following set of tests of coordination abilities for the diagnostics of acquired results in the sport preparation of volleyball (Tab. 5.10).

Test 1: Bench walk with 3 turns
Description: The individual stands behind the 3 m long bench, which is positioned upside down, with their stronger leg up on the edge of the bench. At a signal they stand up on the bench and try to walk to the other side, while making three 360° turns. If they loose balance, they can touch the ground but maximum two times (each touch represents one negative second aded to the final measured time), otherwise

Table 5.10: Motor tests included in the set of coordination tests

Test	Motor task	Coordination ability	Evaluation accuracy
T1 Bench walk with 3 turns	To walk along the bench (3 m) as fast as possible and to perform 3 turns (360°) on the way.	Dynamic balance	Time in sec. (0.01 s)
T2 Stopping the rolling ball	After a 180° turn to stop the rolling ball as soon as possible.	Complex motor reaction	Distance in cm (1 cm)
T3 Movement rythm observation	To remember the specified movement rhythm (rope skipping)	Rhythmic ability	Time in ses. (0.01 s)
T4 Shuttle run	To orientate in space as fast as possible while touching three specified numbered balls.	Space-orientation ability	Time in sec. (0.01 s)
T5 Target standing broad jump	To jump with heels as close as possible to the mark.	Kinesthetic-differentiation ability of legs	Deviation in cm (1 cm)
T6 Target sitting throw	To throw as close as possible to the specified mark.	Differentiation ability of arms	Deviation in cm (1 cm)
T7 Time estimation	To stop the stopwatch as close to the 5 s mark as possible (without watching it)	Estimate of temporal parameters	Deviation in sec. (0.01 s)

they must repeat the test. Time from the starting signal to the touch of the ground behind the bench is measured. One preparatory and two measured attempts.

Test 2: Stopping the rolling ball

Description: 2 benches (5 cm distance between them) are leaned on a shell-board at a height of 120 cm so that a volleball ball can be rolled down between them. On the surface of one of the benches is attached a gauge (meter). Examiner holds a ball at the top of the meter. The individual stands concentrated on a starting line, 150 cm from the lower edge of the benches with theirback to the running direction (they do not watch the ball). The examiner on audio signal allows the ball to roll down the benches gap and the task of the tested person is to stop the ball with both hands as fast as possible. 1 preparatory and 3 measured attempts, the best one is recorded.

Test 3: Movement rhythm observation

Description: Player skips over the rope for 20s in a certain tempo, which they choose. The examiner counts number of rope skips during the given period. In the second part of the test the tested person carries out the same number of skips as in the first part. The examiner measures the time fow which the subject fulfils the task. Deviation from 20s will be the criterion of success in the given test. In the case that the participant makes an error and fails to jump over the rope, he can repeat the test only once. When testing the pupils of elementary school we recommend not to use a skipping rope but to carry out the test only as an imitation of skipping (without a rope).

Test 4: Shuttle run

Description: 6 medicine balls are arranged in the following way: one is in the centre, numbering of the others is free and prior to each measurement we change the positions of the balls. Player starts from the standing position with the back to the balls. Having called one number out of 5 the subject runs to the ball with the called number and touches it, and returns back to touch the ball No. 0. At the moment of touching the 0 ball, the administrator calls another number of the ball (1 to 5). The same is repeated with the third number of a ball. The test finishes with the touching of the ball in the centre after the return from the third ball. Better result out of the two measured times is recorded. One preparatory trial is allowed.

Test 5: Target standing broad jump

Description: Athlete jumps to a maximum distance (2 attempts). After marking the 75% distance of the maximal performance the subject tries to jump forward, landing the heels as close as possible to the given 75% mark. One preparatory and three measured trials. An average of three measured results is recorded.

Test 6: Target sitting throw

Description: On the surface of a playground we stretch a measuring tape (50 m long). The tested person is sitting on the basic line and gradually throws 2 attempts with a tennis ball at the maximum distance. The better result is recorded. In the second part of the test the 50% of the maximum result is marked on the floor. Athlete throws other 10 attempts into the target on the ground. A deviation (absolute value) from the 50% mark is recorded. The level of the measured motor ability is expressed by the average sum of 10 deviations.

Test 7: Time estimation

Description: The tested person at first tries to measure time on a stopwatch. They start the stopwatch and watching the hand try to stop it at the 5 s mark. Then they try to repeat it without any visual control. One preparatory and one measured attempt. Deviation (in sec.) from the 5 s value is measured and recorded.

The majority of the recommended tests (T1-T5 and T7) can be conducted in a gym, indoor, or outside, on a playground. The test T6 of kinesthetic-differentiation ability is an exception. It is administered outside, since it needs a longer area for its realization.

The battery of coordination tests includes those verified by the group of German researchers who stipulated the basic statistical characteristics (reliability, objectiveness, validity and economy) on a sample of approximately 1,300 pupils in age categories from 7 to 24 years. These are tests No.1, 2, 4, 5 and 7. Test No. 3 was described by Dropčová (1987), test No. 6 was taken over from Ljach (1989), who verified it on 1,617 tested persons. Selected characteristics of the test: $r_{stab.}$ = 0.62. Three preparatory and 10 measured trials are recommended.

German authors described these characteristics of the reaction test (T-2): logical (contents) validity: assessed by experts and literary sources, factor validity: 0.48, construct validity: 0.48 - together 0.96 % validity, reliability of the test: (method test-retest): 0.83, objectivity: exactly measurable registration of results. Hirtz (1985) used the test covering space-orientation ability as well as partly also acceleration speed and explosiveness of legs (T-4) under the title Shuttle run. Měkota and Blahuš (1983) revealed test results: $r_{stab.}$ = 0.88 and $r_{obj.}$ = 0.84 while they recommend one preparatory and two measured attempts. Test of differentiation ability of legs is presented by Sehlbach (1988) under the title Target jump down. It is a modification of the test by Měkota and Blahuš (1983). It is important that a feedback is assured after each trial in the tests of differentiation ability.

The test Time estimation (T-7), which was set up by Komárik (1987), captures the ability of the tested person to estimate temporal parameters – to correctly perceive a certain time interval. It records central components of movement control such as motor thinking, motor memory and timing of movements.

5.1.2 Using Standards and Tables

When using the enclosed standards and tables, the following procedure should be observed:
- select a suitable table as to the age and gender of the athlete,
- compare the reached result (performance) with the standards in the particular table gradually in all tests of the battery,
- assess the reached level of the standard and specify the resulting assessment based on the scored number of points for the reached standards in individual tests,
- assess the performance of the player according to his health state, conditions for sport preparation and sport specialization,
- for the recording of test results use the sheet **"Personal trainer of the volleyball player"** (p. 60).

Example: Participant XY is 11 years old and reached the optimum level in all tests and in the test of kinesthetic-differentiation abilities he overcame the limit of top performance standard. That means that he has high prerequisites for such sport game, in which kinesthetic-differentiation abilities are the limiting factor of the structure of sport performance (e.g. basketball, ice-hockey, tennis, and also volleyball). From the point of view of the school sport such individual is evaluated as excellent.

PERSONAL TRAINER OF THE VOLLEYBALL PLAYER
(battery of coordination tests)

Name:	Date of birth:
Body height:	Body weight:
BMI:	Date of testing:

Test - measurement:	Result:	Fulfilment of the norm:
T1: Bench walk with three turns		
T2: Stopping the rolling ball		
T3: Movement rhythm observation		
T4: Shuttle run		
T5: Target standing broad jump		
T6: Target sitting throw		
T7: Time estimation		

Assessment in the tests:

M-minimum level /1 point/

O-optimum level /2 points/

P-performance level /3 points/

Total score of the battery: $B = S1+S2+S3+S4+S5+S6+S7$ = 7-21 points

Difference score: $D = S_{max} - S_{min}$

Total assessment of the battery:

Minimum performance: 7-10 points

Optimum performance: 11-17 points

Competitive performance: 18-21 points

Personal recommendations:

Total level of coordination abilities:

Best developed coordination abilities:

Least developed coordination abilities:

6 Model of Development of Coordination Abilities in Long-Term Sport Preparation in Volleyball

The courses of development of coordination abilities help predict potential growth of specific coordination performance in a particular sport and serve as an example for the need to model coordination preparation in volleyball. Along with increasing coordination demands in elite sport the quality, i.e. technique, skills, and coordination performance of athletes, shall have to be developed.

In sport games, where the level of coordination factors of the sport performance cannot be quantified directly in play, the course of improvement of sport mastery is assessed by means of observing the effectiveness in a game. For example, in volleyball, sport performance is assessed by means of the rate of successful actions in a game. Nowadays, there exists a well developed system of recording and statistical computer processing and assessment of the rate of effectiveness of players in game situations of an individual as well as in group activities. Today, top sport performance directly requires equilibrium and perfect acquisition of technical elements instantaneously.

Effectiveness of the coordination model of preparation can be directly assessed using the given statistics. It shows the degree of realization of the level of individual coordination abilities in motor skills, which decide on the success or failure of action of an individual or a team in a game.

In initial stages of sport preparation the performance itself will not be in the centre of attention of the coaches and players. It is necessary to use the training time in initial stages for the development of coordination abilities. Motor skills should be acquired at first in lightened, later on in standard conditions. After having acquired them, skills can be improved in more complex, hindered conditions and directly in competitive conditions in a game. The timing of increasing the coordination mastery should be so that an athlete reached best parameters in the sphere of conditioning, technique, psychic, but also coordination abilities in an optimum age.

Analysis of coordination abilities in sport games leads to their potential division (Roth, 1982; Hirtz, 1985; Schnabel, 1994) into general coordination prerequisites and special coordination abilities, i.e. those which are limiting for the given sport game. In the initial stages of sport training coaches´ attention should mainly be focused on improving the level of general gross coordination; in the later stages of deepened and highly specialized sport preparation attention should mainly be on specialized coordination abilities, the level of which directly determines their possible effective application in demanding game conditions of a sport match.

It is possible to split the sport preparation in volleyball into a similar division of coordination prerequisites. A basic principle of training coordination abilities is variability of all training methods, while the principle of proceeding from general (overall gross coordination) to particular (special coordination abilities), from easier to more difficult, from simple to complex exercises, is observed. Selection of methods depends on a coach´s creativity, and systematic, planning, goal-oriented work.

"Adaptation changes to specific loading, conditioning an increase in the level of coordination abilities, show a different time flow and that is why it is necessary to plan a specific frequency of stimuli in microcycles, inevitable length of their effect, as well as an optimum size of applied stimuli (specific training loads – their volume and intensity)" (Šimonek & Zrubák, 1995). In order that the effect of the training is manifested on the level of development of coordination abilities, a longer period of time is needed. Experts present at least 8 – 10 weeks and higher frequency of impulses in a microcycle (4 – 6-times a week). Generally speaking, it is necessary to apply 30-50 training units, which will contribute to the solution of all tasks in the given sport game.

Table 6.11 schematically shows the model of development of coordination abilities in sport games in individual stages of the sport preparation.

6.1 Characteristics of Motor Activity in Volleyball

Contemporary top volleyball is characterized by its high level of dynamism, elasticity, economy of movement and fast changes, thus imposing high claims not only on physical preparation, coordination abilities, psychological properties but also spatial vision, fast reaction speed, anticipation, ability to accurately estimate temporal, strength and spatial characteristics of motor activity and also the level of coordination motor prerequisites.

Well-developed coordination abilities positively influence abilities of motor control also in unusual "new" situations. In volleyball, it is enormously important to systematically improve this complex and special ability. An experienced player is very often more successful while blocking or attacking than a younger player who has got a better level of explosiveness and power. The onset of power, muscle strength and direction of strength mean relatively more. Another argument from sport medics is that a player with a well-developed level of motor coordination is less prone to injuries, than a player with poor level of coordination (Schmidt & Lee, 2011).

Rapid situational changes typical of volleyball require players to make quick and accurate assessments of the situation, as well as making fast and effective selection of motor skills for its solution. In volleyball, movement must be corrected until the very last moment, which should bring an optimum result – processing the ball, serve reception, blocking activity, field activity, but also offensive activity, upon which the opponent cannot form its own defense.

Table 6.11: Schematic model of development of coordination abilities in sport games

Model of development	Volleyball	Basketball	Handball	Soccer	Ice-Hockey	Tennis
PŠPS	Age: 10-12 years	Age: 6-8 years	Age: 8-10 years	Age: 7-9 years	Age: 6-9 years	Age: 7-12 years
	Methods of training: repetitive method (mostly 6-12 repetitions in an aerobic regime, heart rate up to 90-100 pulses/min, interval of rest: until full recovery), contrast method (e.g. changing of faster and slower tempo of performing exercises), graduation method (increasing the speed of performance of movements), method of variable exercises (performing exercises under hindered/unfavoured conditions, variability), method of gradual increasing the demand is of exercises, "freshness" method (performing exercises at the beginning of a training unit), method using complementary exercises (e.g. a combination of requirements of differentiation of the way of ball rotation with the differentiation of direction of the ball), method of special focus of an exercise (focused only on a single coordination ability), game method (with modified rules), method of performing exercises in lightened conditions (focused on technique), "firing" method (e.g. from jogging quickly react to a signal) and others. Loading: Intensity is low, duration 10-15´					
ISŠŠ	Age: 13-14 years	Age: 9-12 years	Age: 11-14 years	Age: 10-12 years	Age: 10-14 years	Age: 13-14 years
	Methods of training: repetitive method (smaller number of repetitions, several times a day, 4-6x weekly), method of generalized exercise (with the overall influence on several coordination abilities), method of variation of information reception (e.g. through a hindered visual analyser), method of variation of apparatuses and tools (e.g. various size of a ball), competitive method, method of strictly specified variation, fartlek ("play with speed ") and many others. Loading: Intensity is medium, duration 15-25´					
ŠŠPS	Age: 15-17 years	Age: 13-17 years	Age: 15-19 years	Age: 13-18 years	Age: 15-18 years	Age: 15-16 years
	Methods of training: method "under fatigue" (performing exercises under fatigue), method of "mirror" exercises, method of irritating vestibular apparatus, method of joined effect (development of coordination abilities parallely executed with the improvement of sport technique), method of free tactical variation (realization of various tactical tasks with different teammates and opponents), ideomotoric method (perception of temporal, spatial and dynamic parameters of movement prior to performing exercises), method of executing exercises in hindered conditions, and others. Loading: Intensity is submaximum to maximum (with longer rest intervals), duration 25-30´.					

Explanations: PSPS - stage of pre-sport preparation, ISSS - stage of initial sport specialization, SSPS - stage of specialized sport preparation

6.2 Factors Limiting Sport Performance in Volleyball

Game performance in volleyball includes highly complex reactions with a choice of a suitable response, which closely depend on the processes of reception and processing information, therefore, it is obvious that coordination abilities, as relatively lasting, generalized performance prerequisites for programming, controlling and rectifying of movements are immensely important factors of the structure of sport performance in volleyball (Tab. 6.12, 6.13, Fig. 6.5).

If we add to the 15% share of coordination abilities also a partial share of fast reaction speed abilities, we reach a rather important share (up to 30%) of coordination abilities on the whole performance of a volleyball player. Understandably, the importance of individual coordination abilities changes with the player´s postion, e.g.in a setter, a high level of kinesthetic-differentiation ability of arms is expected, while in a receiving player and defensive player there is an assumption of a faster reaction speed to the spiked ball.

Table 6.12: Share of components of movement potential on the sport performance in volleyball (Mangi, Jokl & Dayton, 1987)

Components	Points
Aerobic endurance	2
Speed abilities	3
Power abilities	2
Anaerobic endurance	2
Flexibility	3
Coordination abilities	3

Explanations: Scale points from 1 to 4.

Table 6.13: Share of components of movement potential (conditional and coordination abilities) on the performance in volleyball (Jonath & Krempel, 1991)

Components	Share
Speed abilities	15%
Power abilities	45%
Endurance abilities	10%
Flexibility	15%
Coordination abilities	15%

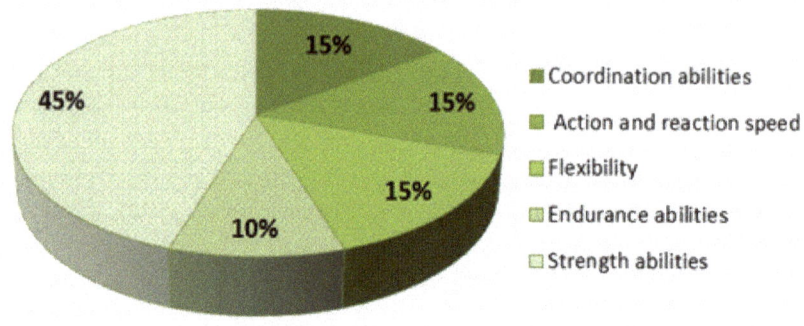

Fig. 6.5: Most important factors of structure of the sport performance in volleyball (Letzelter, 1978)

Acquisition of game activities and their further improvement and consecutive application in a game, is the task of the long-term training effort, which assumes employment of a rational selection of various training means and methods, as well as a satisfactory frequency of optimum training loads.

Research into volleyball theory and practice (Zimmermann, 1982; Dannemann, 1985) shows that the most decisive for volleyball are mostly reaction speed (specifically complex motor reaction with a choice), then kinesthetic-differentiation ability of legs (ability to estimate explosive strength) and kinesthetic-differentiation ability of arms (ability to estimate strength of ball hitting, upon passing or spiking), especially of setters.

Zimmermann (1982) specified the following ranking of coordination abilities for volleyball:

Reaction speed	30 points
Kinesthetic-differentiation	28 points
Space-orientation	27 points
Coupling and binding of movements	20 points
Motor activity rebuilding	18 points
Rhythmic ability	13 points
Balance ability	12 points

Dannemann (1985) presents importance of individual coordination abilities from the point of view of acquisition of motor skills (game activities of an individual) in Table 6.14. Let us characterize individual displays of coordination abilities in a volleyball game. Motor reaction is one of the most important abilities in volleyball. It can be defined as coordination-motoric prerequisite of a player for fast beginning and realization of effective short-term movement activities executed to an external stimulus (signal or change of situation). A volleyball player must react to stimuli of

Table 6.14. Importance of coordination abilities from the point of view of sport-technical skills in volleyball (Dannemann, 1985)

Coordination ability	Motor skill					
	Serve	Underhand reception	Overhand pass	Spike	Blocking	Field play
Raction speed	-	3	1	1	3	3
Differentiation	2	2	3	2	-	3
Orientation	2	2	2	2	2	2
Coupling	1	2	2	2	2	2
Balance	1	1	1	2	2	2
Rebuilding	-	2	1	2	1	2
Rhythmic	1	1	1	1	1	1

Explanations: Point scale from 1 (min. value) to 3 (max. value) according to the importance from the point of view of a sport skill

various kinds: acoustic (shout of a team-mate or opponent) or optic (sign, movement), expected (signal for serving) or unexpected ones (change of activity of a spiker from spiking into lobbing or faking). Also internal stimuli impact the coordination of a player: kinesthetic information upon ball touching through muscles, vestibular information – sense of balance, tactile information – through skin (touch). Prior to the signal, a volleyball player has got enough time for the preparation (serve reception), however, more frequently he is under a time pressure (block upon fast spike).

In volleyball simple motor or complex motor reaction are applied. Upon simple motor reaction only a part of the body is moving (only a special part of muscles is involved in the movement) and the player responds to an expected signal by a standard movement. However, in practice we often meet with a complex motor reaction when the player responds in the shortest possible time, while there exist several stimuli. Sometimes player must react to just one stimulus, which offers several possible answers and there is the need to choose the most adequate one to the given situation. The player reacts to a moving object (ball, opponent, team-mate) and attempts the fastest choice leading to a success. A ball spiked by an opponent approaches the receiving player, standing on the service line in 0.33s (in female volleyball in 0.5s) and the reaction speed of trained individuals reaches about 0.35s. Evidently, to successfully catch the ball requires more than just fast reactions but also the ability of anticipation, i.e. presumption based on available information on the course of the play. A player´s experience impacts anticipation ability in terms of detemining initial

position of the opponent, preparatory movements, as well as overall game situation and knowledge of an opponent´s habits. Specifically in volleyball, reaction speed is important mainly for:
- catching the spike (flight speed of a ball is over 100 km/hod – Schnabel & Thiess, 1993),
- blocking (if the opponent changes the direction of a spike suddenly),
- serve reception (speed of ball flight reaches 20 m/s),
- field play (fake, deflected ball from the net, block, touched ball),
- setting (sudden change of direction of the flight of the set ball, according to the reaction of blockers).

It is commonly accepted that the development of straight-line sprinting ability is important for track-and-field athletes who participate in other field- or court-based sports (e.g. soccer, American football, baseball) (Sheppard & Young, 2006). This type of speed is developed by drills and activities that target acceleration, maximal speed, and speed endurance (Plisk, 2008). Although the ability to react quickly, rapidly accelerate is an important skill, the athlete must also be able to rapidly change direction in response to the sporting environment. All this applies also to volleyball. *Agility* training in volleyball includes rapid movements with the decision-making processes.

In volleyball, the ability to control movements in time and space is an inevitable coordination ability, which is externally manifested in accuracy and economy of movements in spite of time stress, defensive activity of the opponent and frequently also of fatigue. It requires conscious and perfect synchronization of movement with motor visualization. Kinesthetic differentiation in volleyball allows for:
- accurate and timed (to a certain height, zone, by a certain speed and under a cartain angle) pass from the setter to the spiker,
- accurate second pass through an overhead pass by the field player to the setter,
- accurate reception of the ball by the field player (underhand pass) – first pass,
- accurately placed serve,
- correctly timed jump up of the spiker upon spiking,
- correctly timed jump up of the blocker upon blocking,
- placed and timed dink, tip attack.

For a volleball player, the *"feeling of ball"* by hands is characteristic; mainly in a setter it represents a very important component of performance. *Kinesthetic-differentiation ability* plays a special role especially in the stage of improvement and stabilization of sport movements, as well as upon their application in a game activity in a match. According to some authors (Kollárovits & Gerhát, 1993; Šimková & Ramacsay, 1993) sensoric abilities (space-orientation and kinesthetic-differentiation ability to estimate time, space and strength) are limited also by genetic factors, however, they can be improved by the training.

Space-orientation ability is related to the functions of analyzers (visual, acoustic, kinesthetic, tactile and vestibular) and also motor experience. It represents an ability to accurately and quickly estimate position of the body or its parts in relation to the external environment (limitation of the playground by lines, team-mates, opponent, ball, net). It allows the player to correctly orientate oneself in a game situation and coordinate movements in compliance with the particular motor task. It is employed mostly for:
- faking (faking activity) by running-in spikers (signals),
- observing and playing the ball by a setter to the best positioned spiker, or upon tip attack,
- spiking (spiker) through a "gap" in badly positioned opponent´s defense (blocks),
- stopping the opponent´s offensive activity by means of a successful "positioning" of hands on a block,
- correct field layout upon serve reception and a successful reception of the ball in the field.

From the analysis of game situations in volleyball, as well as available resources (Zimmermann, 1982; Dannemann, 1985; Brandt, 1985) we suggest the following model of the structure of coordination abilities participating in the sport performance in volleyball (Fig. 6.6).

6.3 Periodization of the Contents of Sport Preparation in Volleyball

The system of long-term sport preparation of young talented volleyball players represents a chain of rational, coupled elements or stages of preparation, joined into one whole. It is a long-term, purposeful and optimum action at young talented players and forming their characteristic traits. Key problems in the preparation of young volleyball players is differentiation of the whole training season into individual sections or stages. Based on the long-term practical experience, as well as conclusions from research, the long-term sport preparation in volleyball can be devided into (Zeleznjak, 1988):
- stage of sport pre-preparation (10-12 years),
- stage of preliminary sport specialization (13-14 years),
- stage of deepened sport specialization (15-17 years),
- stage of top sport preparation (18 and over).

All the stages form a unified whole, however, each stage has certain specified tasks and objectives, related to age, level of trainability, participation in competition. In the stage of sport pre-preparation the coach is aimed at fair motivation and attracting attention of children in playing volleyball, but also regular trainings using general means in order to support health and develop his optimum psychic and somatic

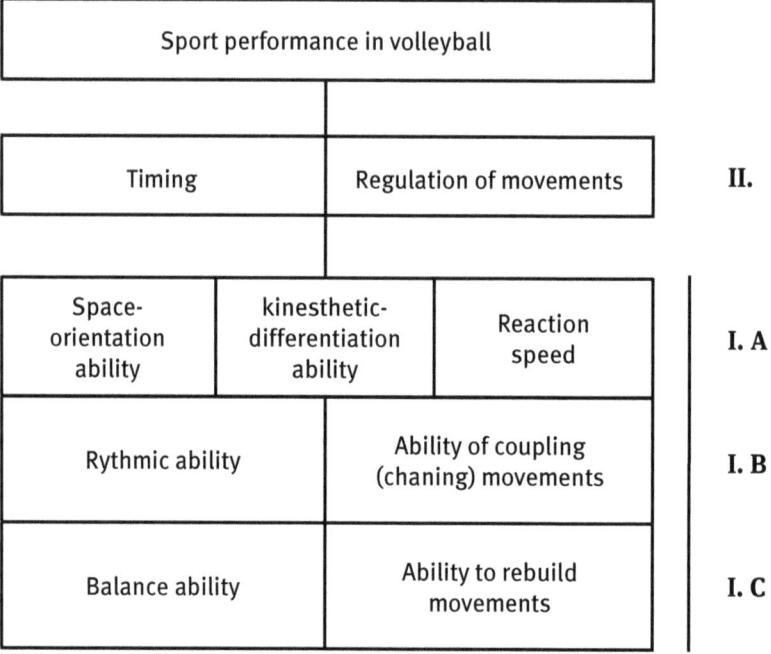

Fig. 6.6: Model of the structure of coordination abilities participating in the performance of a volleyball player. **Explanations:** II. - level of special coordination abilities, which directly limit sport performance in volleyball. I. A - level of general coordination abilities. I. B - coordination abilities directly limiting sport performance. I. C - coordination abilities important from the point of view of sport performance, but compensable - less important coordination abilities

growth. In the stage of preliminary sport specialization rudiments of rational sport technique and tactic, which, however, are built on the acquired platform of general preparation, begin to be acquired. In this stage, coaches should avoid a premature narrow specialization (gradually go through all offensive and defensive posts in the team) and widen as much as possible, the set of technical skills of young volleyball players. A pupil´s sport age is the most important one for acquiring all abilities, which are inevitable for a successful athlete (Tab. 6.15).

At the beginning of the stage of specialized sport preparation, narrower specialization of players into posts begins along with a gradual increase in the volume and intensity of training load (often to the maximum); sport technique but also tactics are on a high level depending on the sport specialization (spiker, blocker, setter). Sport training in this stage is governed by the principles of specialized universality, increasing the load and complexity (Choutka & Dovalil, 1991).

Table 6.15: Share of individual kinds of sport preparation in the total volume of preparation in sport schools with the focus on volleyball (Ajrijanc & Klešcev, 1985)

	Stage of sport pre-preparation (10-12 years):		
1.	Theoretical preparation	-	18 hrs
2.	Overall physical preparation	-	126 hrs
3.	Special sport preparation	-	65 hrs
4.	Technical preparation	-	100 hrs
5.	Tactical preparation	-	53 hrs
6.	Matches	-	34 hrs
7.	Tests, control exercises	-	20 hrs

Total: 416 hours for a year of sport preparation

The process of education of top volleyball players is accomplished in the stage of top sport preparation, when athletes reach excellent results and performance on the top limit of their possibilities.

Upon solving the tasks of planning of the training process the important role is played by forecasting and modelling of sport preparation. Since Slovak volleyball players do not reach top world performance at this time, it is necessary that coaches stick to comparative attitude to model characteristics of athletes of those countries which currently play best at international level. The most problematic sphere is registration of indicators, characterizing individual factors of sport performance. Prognoses of performance development (partial models in individual stages of preparation) in volleyball shall become important predictors of the direction the training process shall follow in the nearest future.

6.4 Methodology for the Development of Coordination Abilities in Volleyball

Our model of coordination preparation in volleyball will consist of incorporation of coordination component (block of special exercises focused at the development of coordination abilities) into physical preparation (conditioning) in individual stages of sport preparation. The share of coordination preparation in the total volume of loading will be changing from stage to stage, as far as the amount and quality are concerned. Table 6.16 shows basic indicators of the training programme in the period of initial sport preparation.

In the stage of initial sport preparation children start to acquire first habits of games, initial selection continues – it is a selection of children for volleyball, a permanent

Table 6.16: Share of individual kinds of preparation in the year's cycle of the first, second and third years of sport preparation (in hours) (according to Zeleznjak, 1988)

Kinds of sport preparation	4th year of sport preparation				6th year of sport preparation			
	Without concentration training	With concentration training			Without concentration training	With concentration training		
		Total for year 1	During the school year	At the concentration training		Total for year 1	During the school year	At the concentration training
Theoretical	8	8	8	-	14	14	14	-
General conditioning	86	86	76	10	112	112	92	20
Special conditioning	52	58	48	10	58	72	56	16
Technical	76	94	70	24	94	122	88	34
Tactical	26	30	22	8	48	54	44	10
Integral	26	32	22	10	34	38	24	14
Number of competition days	12	15	12	3	20	20	16	4
Testing	14	14	10	4	16	16	10	6
Number of training hours:	312	352	280	72	416	468	360	108
Number of training days	144	161	128	33	188	196	164	32
Number of training units	144	161	128	33	188	214	164	50
Number of of working days	156	176	140	36	208	220	180	36

interest in volleyball training process is developing. The place of coordination preparation can be found in three elementary spheres of sport preparation: in general (86 hours in the first and second years, and 112 in the third year of sport preparation) and specialized (52 hours in the first and second years, and 58 in the third year of sport preparation) sport preparation and in technical preparation (76 hours in the first and second years and 94 in the third year of sport preparation).

The content of general sport preparation will be exercises focused on general development of all basic coordination abilities inevitable for the later sport specialization. Part of the special sport preparation will be focused development of those coordination abilities, which are limiting for volleyball – reaction, kinesthetic-differentiation and space-orientation. Development of coordination abilities is also a part of technical improvement and therefore coaches should pay an increased attention to acquisition of correct technical elements of performing movements in the initial sport preparation. Various methods of development of coordination abilities are employed here, such as: improvement of motor skills in changed conditions, their bilateral acquisition (performing exercises on both sides – with left and right hands) In the *first year of sport preparation* coordination component should form more than 50% of the total time assigned for physical preparation. We shall present just a few examples of training units with various focus.

Training unit No. 1 (1st year of training in a sport club): Development of reaction speed
Tasks: Development of simple motor reaction
Duration of the unit: 90 minutes

Preparatory part – 20 minutes – contents: Selection from the exercises stated below:
1. Players A and B face each other, arms bent, palms turned up, fingers are close together. Task of player A is to clap the palms of player B as quickly as possible. Player B can dodge. If player A did not hit the palm of the opponent, it becomes Player B's turn to clap.
2. Players A and B face each other in a low stance, hands on outer sides of thighs by the body. Player A tries to pull out the "gun" and "shoot" at player B, who tries to prevent player A from shooting by means of clapping on the "pistol" of player A. If player B succeed, it becomes Player B´s turn to "pull the gun".
3. Player A holds a gymnastic stick by its upper end in a vertical direction. Player B stands or kneels in front of him and holds his arm so that his forearm is bent in front of the body (90 degrees) and fingers are encircling the lower end of the stick, however, they are not touching it. When A drops the stick, B must catch it. On the stick there is marked a gauge in centimeters, which measures the level of reaction ability (change of execution – the opposite hand).
4. A couple of players, facing each other. Player A holds a ball in her arms stretched forward and suddenly drops it. The task of player B is to catch it before it touches the ground.

5. A couple of players. Player A faces the wall in a 3-5 m distance. B throws a ball from behind player A onto the wall and player A tries to catch it and put it on the floor after a bounce from the wall. The game can be made more difficult by implementing more balls.
6. Couples of players in a queue, 5-8 m distance. On a signal of the trainer, back player throws the ball towards the teammate standing in the front of the queue. The front player attempts at turning round on a signal and catch the ball. Then the players change their positions.
7. Coach shouts body positions (e.g. sitting, lying at the back, kneeling, side lying, squatting, etc.) in a fast sequence. Players try to occupy the positions as fast as possible, to execute a jump up and return to the initial standing position.
8. Starts from various positions (sit, lying position, kneeling position, etc.) on a signal of a different character (audible, visual).
9. Player B stands 2 m behind player A. Player A, on a signal of the trainer, throws the ball to the right and left of the player B, who attempts at catching it after a turn sooner than it falls on the ground.
10. 5-6 players standing in a semi-circle (distances 4-5 m), each with a ball. They gradually throw the ball in a fast sequence to the player, who is standing in front of them in a distance of 6 - 8 m. Her task is to catch/bounce back as many balls as possible. We can make the play more difficult by numbering the players. The coach shouts number of the player, who has to pass to the central player.

Main part – 65 minutes – contents: Acquisition of low position, overhand passing.
Closing part – 5 minutes – contents: jogging, walking and deep breathing, conclusion of the reached results, motivation into further training work.

Training unit No. 2 (1st year of training in a sport club):
Development of reaction speed
Tasks: Development of complex motor reaction ability
Duration of the unit: 90 minutes

Preparatory part – 20 minutes – contents: Selection of the exercises shown below:
1. Players freely move on the playground and on an acoustic signal they have to carry out a certain task (sit, 360 degrees turn, etc).
2. 5 gymnastic rings are situated on the floor of the volleyball playground and 6 jogging players move around it. On a signal, each player attempts at occupying a place in the ring. Player, who has not succeeded in it, is punished by 1 penalty point. The game continues until 10 points are scored or certain time elapses.
3. Two to four marked "fishermen" try to catch other players. If the fisherman touches any player, he must stop at a place with his legs spread apart. Free player can free him by passing through his legs wide apart.
4. Two players facing each other lay their arms on each other´s shoulders. They try to step on the foot of the opponent.

5. Two players facing each other, while being partitioned by a volleyball net. Player A does some activities by the net (squat, jump up, blocking, spiking, side gallop, etc.), player B tries to react as fast as possible and repeat the activity of player A.
6. Players A and B standing on baselines of the opposed sides of the playground. Player A has a ball and serves it over the net, player B tries to catch it before it touches the ground.
7. 5-6 players are standing freely on a half of the the playground with their backs towards the net. Player A, who is standing with balls on the other side of the net, serves the ball on a trainer´s signal to the opponent, who attempts at catching/bouncing the ball after a turn and start a rally.
8. Serving/playing around the net, which is hidden by a large piece of cloth.
9. Standing player A: feet slightly apart, arms stretched forward (ball on waist level). He throws up the ball hair high, claps his hands on his thighs (behind the body, touching the ground, repeatedly claps his hands in front of his waist, etc.) and catches the ball again at waist level. Organize a game, the winner is the most skilled player.
10. A couple of players standing with their backs together. A skipping rope is spread between their legs apart (handles of the rope are at feet level, between them). On a signal of the coach each player attempts at pulling the rope by its handles faster than the opponent.

Main part – 65 minutes – contents: Underhand passing drill, improvement of overhead passing.

Closing part – 5 minutes – contents: jogging, walking and deep breathing, conclusion of results reached, motivation into further training work.

Training unit No. 3 (2nd year of training in a sport club):
Technical and tactical preparation.
Tasks: Improvement of passing accuracy (while standing and running-in).
Development of kinesthetic-differentiation ability of arms
Duration of the unit: 90 minutes

Preparatory part – 20 minutes – contents: Selection of the exercises:
Passing or throwing of balls of different size and weight (tennis, cricket, handball, volleyball balls) on a target at a distance of 3-6 m.
1. A trio of players with balls. Two of them (A and B) face each other at a distance of 6-8 m, player C stands in between. They pass/throw the ball quickly as to the pattern: B-A, A-C, C-B. After a certain time interval they exchange their positions. Repeat 15-20 times.
2. Players stand in a queue (2-3 m apart). Player A stands 3-5 m in front of the player B, in a queue, and she gradually exchanges a pass with all the players from the queue, while all move by one position. After a pass the player makes a squat.
3. The same as in drill 5 but with calling the numbers of players. All players are in

a squat and the player, whose number the trainer shouts, stands up, receives the ball and passes it back to the central player.
4. A player passes the ball above and does a 90, 180, 360-degree turn.
5. A couple of players facing each other at a distance of 4-6 m. Player A passes the ball to player B, who, before passing the ball back, lays his ball down on the floor or passes it above his head. The action repeats.
6. Two teams try to pass the ball using an overhead pass into the circle at a distance of 6-8 m. The team, which reaches higher number of hits for a time interval, wins.
7. Basket-shooting. Two teams of equal number of players face their own basket at a distance of 4-6 m. Each player has a ball. The players, one by one, attempt at passing the ball to the basket.
8. Overhead passing while walking and pushing another ball with a leg.
9. A trio of players, one having a ball, stands in a triangle. Each has a medicine-ball on the floor at a distance of 2-3 m behind them. The player with the ball passes to the partner to the right, makes a start, touches his medicine-ball and quickly returns back to his initial position before he receives a pass from player 3. Passes should be performed so fast that the partner is not able to fulfil the task.

Main part – 65 minutes – contents: Improvement of passing accuracy while standing and running. Improvement of both handed underhand and overhand passing (stress on accuracy).

Closing part – 5 minutes – contents: trotting, walking and deep breathing, conclusions of the obtained results, motivation for further training work.

Individual kinds of sport preparation **in the stage of initial specialization have** different proportion: technical preparation (25%), tactical preparation (18%) and integral preparation-game (21%). Table 6.17 presents the portion of individual kinds of sport preparation on the total volume of preparation in the period of initial sport specialization and in the period of specialized training.

We present model examples of microcycles with various contents part of which also includes the development of coordination abilities and improvement of technical skills.

Example of a training unit in the microcycle in the 6th year of training process
(9th week of preparatory period):
Tasks: Development of kinesthetic-differentiation ability
Duration of the unit: 90 minutes

Preparatory part – 30 minutes – contents: Selection of exercises:
1. Passing or throwing of balls of a different size and weight (tennis, cricket, basketball, volleyball, mini-volleyball, handball, small medicine-ball) onto a target from a distance of 3-9 meters.
2. Passing of balls to distant targets (e.g. gradually pass 5 balls with an effort to hit the full balls put in irregular distances).

Table 6.17: Share of individual kinds of preparation in a year's cycle of the fourth through eighth year of sport preparation (in hours) (according to Zeleznjak, 1988)

Kinds of sport preparation	4th year of sport preparation				6th year of sport preparation				8th year of sport preparation			
	Without concentration training	With concentration training			Without concentration training	With concentration training			Without concentration training	With concentration training		
		Total for a year	During the school year	At the concentration training		Total for a year	During the school year	At the concentration training		Total for a year	During the school year	At the concentration training
Theoretical	20	22	18	4	30	34	30	4	38	44	40	4
General conditioning	80	120	86	34	110	126	108	18	143	104	86	18
Special conditioning	86	102	80	22	124	136	110	26	154	140	122	18
Technical	106	126	98	28	164	168	144	24	192	206	182	24
Tactical	58	74	58	16	122	130	110	20	150	170	152	18
Games	68	84	64	22	120	128	104	24	150	200	176	24
Number of competition days	24	24	20	4	44	44	36	8	55	55	45	10
Testing	20	20	16	4	18	18	16	2	24	26	22	4
Number of training hours	520	608	470	136	832	888	744	144	1040	1079	935	144
Number of training days	188	204	172	32	220	228	200	28	215	226	200	26
Number of training units	188	236	172	64	264	300	236	64	360	422	360	62

3. A trio of players with balls. Two players face each other at a distance of 10-12 m, player C stands between them. They pass the ball quickly according to the pattern: B-A, A-C, C-B. After a certain time interval they exchange their positions. Repeat 15-20 times.
4. Passing the ball to the wall so that it falls, after rebounding, to a certain zone marked on the floor at a distance of 3-5 m from the wall.
5. Players stand in a queue (2-3 m behind each other). Player A stands 3-5 m in front of the queue and gradually exchanges a pass with the first through the last players, while all move one position. After a pass the player makes a squat.
6. The same as in drill 5 but with calling the numbers of players. All players are in a squat and the player, whose number the trainer shouts, stands up, receives the ball and passes it back to the central player.
7. Player A with a ball behind the basic line. Other players with a ball are situated irregularly on the playground (each in a different distance from player A). Player A gradually exchanges a pass with all players. Players shift by 1 position in the direction of watch hands.
8. Repeated both-legged leaps with landing into marked zones in various distances from each other.
9. Standing broad jums to a marked line at various distances (200 cm, 210 cm, 220 cm).
10. Passing the ball overhead while standing and after a pass make a 90, 180 and 360-degree turn.
11. Squatting vaults over 5-6 obstacles of various heights (hurdles, gymnastic bucks, vaulting boxes pieces, benches, medicine-balls).
12. A couple facing each other standing at a distance of 6-8 m. Player A passes to player B, who, before passing the ball back, lays his ball down on the floor or passes it above her head. The action repeats.
13. A couple of players standing at a distance of 6-9 m, each having a ball. They simultaneously pass the balls, while player B consistently changes his position (moves forward and backward). Players exchange their roles.
14. Two teams of equal number of players try to hit the circle situated on the floor at a distance of 10-15 m. Team, which gains more hits at a certain time interval, wins.
15. Basket-shooting. Two teams of equal number of players face their own basket at a distance of 4-6 m. Each player has a ball. The players, one by one, attempt at passing the ball to the basket.
16. Overhead passing in a circle with one player standing in the centre. Six players form a circle with a radius of 4-6 m. 7th player stands in the centre with three balls which she gradually passes to the game. Marking of players: A – central player, B,C,D,E,F,G – players standing on the circumference of the circle. Ball trajectory: A- pases the first ball to B, who passes it to C and C returns it back to A. A passes the second ball to D and D to E and E back to A. A passes the third ball to player F, who passes it to G and G back to A. Players attempt at realizing the passes as soon

as possible so that the central player was under time pressure and could not catch all the three balls and put them on the floor.
17. Two players standing in queues facing each other at a distance of 5-7 m. On a signal the first player of team A passes an overhead pass to the first player of team B and runs to the end of the opponent queue. First player of team B passes the ball back to the first player of the opponent team and runs to the end of the opponent team. You can modify the distance of passing.
18. Repeated passing of the ball overhead while walking and at the same time pushing the ball with one leg (also in the form of a slalom between medicine-balls).
19. A couple standing on two benches standing one behind the other at a distance of 3-6 m. Overhead passing in a couple while players change their positions forward and backward.
20. Players form a circle with a radius of 3-5 m, each with a ball. In the centre, there stands one player without a ball. Players standing on the circle around her gradually pass their balls to her in order to put her under stress. Changing the centre player after a while.
21. A trio of players is standing in a triangle, one having a ball. Each of them has a medicine-ball on the floor at a distance of 2-3 m behind them. Player with a ball passes the partner to the right, makes a start, touches his medicine-ball and quickly returns back to his initial position before he receives a pass from player 3. Passes should be performed so fast that the partner was not able to fulfil the task.
22. Two players facing each other. Each of them has a ball. Overhead passing with two balls. Modification – playing with three balls.
23. Overhead passing with dark spectacles (with eyes half shut).
24. Lines are drawn on the wall in a different height (220, 230, 260, 280, 290, 305, 320 cm). Player with a ball faces the wall at a distance of 2-4 meters. Passing the ball into the marked zones (coach shouts numbers of zones).
25. A horizontal line at the height of 220 cm is drawn into a corner of the gym (both left and right). Player with a ball faces the corner approx. at the distance of 2-3 m. He gradually passes the first ball to the right over the line and second ball to the left over the line.
26. Players stand with their side to the wall and facing each other. Overhead passing in couples so that the ball bounces from the wall (the basket).
27. Both legged splits over parts of the vaulting box situated on the ground, while player jumps into each of the component parts, which are spaced irregularly.
28. Mark 5 lines in various heights on the wall. Repeated jumping with reaching the lines with numbers shouted by the trainer.

Some drills for athletic adults and youngsters to consider when they desire **to improve hand eye coordination** for the sake of sports performance (according to Rousseau, 2013):

29. Connect Four: Connect Four is a game of visual planning and organization. The hand part of hand eye coordination won't get much of a workout. However, the eye part will and that can't hurt.
30. Focus near and far: Quickly practice focusing on a near and then a far object. Go back and forth, back and forth.
31. Have someone try to throw a soft ball (like a nerf ball) by you into a real or makeshift goal. The only catch? You have to stop the ball with your hands. Depending on your performance, have the thrower move closer or further away.
32. Have a catch with a catch: Get a large wiffle ball, softball, or really any ball that's light colored. Then write a bunch of letters on the ball with a black marker. Next, find someone to have a catch with. As each of you is about to catch the ball, call out the last letter you see.
33. Have a catch with yourself: One thing you can do to improve hand eye coordination is throw a baseball up in the air repeatedly and catch it. The same goes for any ball, including a football.
34. Raquet sports: Try playing as many raquet sports as possible. Ever play ping pong? Well, if you have then you know how much that sport can improve your hand eye coordination. Have to assume that raquetball is of the same ilk. Tennis too. In other words, anytime you have to react to another person's movement and a ball with your own hand, you're going to improve hand eye coordination.
35. Speed bag drills: Boxers have outstanding hand eye coordination simply because if they didn't they'd be unconscious a lot of the time. One thing they do to keep sharp is use the speed bag.
36. Video games: Chris Spielman, an outstanding former linebacker for the Detroit Lions, once indicated that he sometimes would work on hand eye coordination via video games. How often this occurred is unclear. What we do know is that visual perception and motor skills can be improved through the use of video games.
37. Wall ball: Stand in front of a flat wall with a basketball. Then begin to throw it against the wall and catch it. After you've warmed up sufficiently, begin to throw it against the wall with only one hand. Every time it bounces off the wall push it back against the wall - without catching it - with the fingertips of the same hand you threw it with. Then repeat with your non-dominant hand.

Example of a training unit in the microcycle in the sixth year of training process

(20th week of competition period)
Tasks: Development of space-orientation ability
Duration of the unit: 90 minutes

Preparatory part – 30 minutes – contents: Selection of the following exercises:
1. Playing over the net with a smaller/larger number of players with two balls at once.
2. 6 players stand with their backs to the net in low stance on a volleball field. On a signal player A standing behind the base line of the opponent's ground serves

the ball. Players in the field react to the signal, make a 180° turn, catch the ball and realize an attacking combination according to the number the coach shouts. Position of players in the field is changing after several serves.

3. Team stands in a queue and in front of the first player there is a mat. Player A with a ball stands opposite her team approx. 4-5 m from it. First player of the team makes a front roll, passes the ball to player A, and replaces her. Player A runs to the end of the queue. All players from the queue gradually exchange themselves.
4. Hunting game on a small field with a large number of players and several marked hunters.
5. Players spike a ball to the floor so that it bounced from the wall above them in order to spike again. Repeat 15-20 times in two to three series.
6. Player passes the ball high above his head and after each pass he makes a 180 (360 degree) turn. 3 series 10 passes each.
7. Overhead passing in couples and after each pass the players make a 180-360 degree turn or squat, kneel, sit, lying position.
8. Overhead passing in couples at various distances and later also with more balls.
9. Exercises in trios. Player in the centre makes a turn to player A or B and passes underhand or overhand pass.
10. The same as in drill 9 but the player in the centre passes the ball in turns after a front roll (player A) and a back roll (player B).
11. Two teams (A and B) are freely spaced on each half of the playground, while each player of team A has a ball. Players move freely around the playground while passing their balls above their heads. Each player of team A has a partner in team B. On a signal players of team A quickly orientate themselves and pass the ball to their partner at the other side of the net, who continues in overhead passing while moving. Repeat 10 times.
12. Two players facing, each at the playground's width. They pass the ball repeatedly while galloping sideways. After a pass they carry out a 360 degree turn.
13. Players stand in two queues facing each other. On a signal the first player of team A passes an overhead pass to the first player of team B and runs to the end of the opponent queue. First player of team B passes the ball back to the first player of the opponent team and runs to the end of the opponent team. You can modify the distance of passing.
14. A team stands in a queue behind the base line. In front of these players 3 mats in a row are situated at the distance of 3 m, behind them there are 3 balls on the floor. Setter B stands at a distance of 6-9 m from the balls. On a signal, the first player (A) of the team starts forward, makes 3-4 front rolls (back rolls, alternatively, front and back), takes one ball and passes it to the setter B, who catches it and puts it on the floor. Player A runs back to the base line, touches it and repeats rolls and passes the ball to the setter until all 4 balls have been passed. Relay continues with other players (team's game).
15. Players with numbers 1-5 stand in a circle around the player 6 (stands in the centre). On a signal player 6 passes the ball to the player with the ball shouted

by the coach(eg. 1,4,3,1,2). Player in the circle passes the ball back to the central player.
16. Six players with balls stand in a circle with a radius of 3 m. On a signal, they pass the ball above head and pass it to the player standing on the right. They peripherally watch other balls so as one player has not got two balls at once.
17. Team in a queue behind the base line. 5-6 numbered players are freely spaced on the ground. Player A occupies a low stance at a distance of 2-3 m in front of the line. He receives gradually fast passes from the players in the queue and passes to the plyer on the ground, whose number is shouted by the coach. After a certain number of passes players exchange their roles.
18. Circuit training, where a player makes alternatively various activities like overhead pass and front roll (back roll, cartwheel, a 180 degree turn, jump up for blocking, back dive, front dive).

In the stage of top sport preparation, we expect satisfactorily developed mastery in players, which is based on a high level of coordination abilities. It is manifested by a virtuous, athletic acquisition of skills by an individual as well as in cooperation in a game. A characteristic sign is effectiveness of individual game situations in individual matches in volleyball. Coordination preparation is focused on improving the quality of the level of special coordination abilities, which are tweaked in the process of technical improvement (Tab. 6.18). We provide an example of a microcycle in the tenth year of sport preparation (Tab. 6.19).

Table 6.18: Share of individual kinds of preparation in a year´s cycle of the nineth to eleventh year of sport preparation (in hours) (according to Zeleznjak, 1988)

Kinds of sport preparation	Year of training preparation		
	9.	10.	11.
Theoretical	46	50	60
General conditioning	110	110	130
Special conditioning	140	140	180
Technical	200	245	260
Tactical	200	200	250
Games	208	242	290
Testing	30	32	36
Number of training hours:	1144	1248	1456
▪ number of training days	258	276	276
▪ number of training units	374	398	408
▪ number of working days	60	65	70

Table 6.19: Example of a microcycle in the tenth year of sport preparation (second stage of preparatory period)

Day	Contents of sport preparation	Load proportioning
Monday	**Morning**: Development of coordination abilities and strength. Exercises should be focused on the development of reaction speed, space-orientation ability and explosiveness (rope-skipping and obstacle leaping). **Afternoon**: Development of speed abilities – sprinting exercises, starts from various positions, stretching	20 min. Gymnastic exercises 6-7 exercises, 3-4x 10 for each coordination ability 10x 10 m from low start, 20 repetitions of reaction exercises
Tuesday	**Morning**: Development of aerobic endurance – continuous steady run in the nature, interval running, stretching	600-800 m run, warm-up, 3x 600 m tempo run
Wednesday	**Morning**: Development of coordination and strength abilities. Coordination exercises focused on the development of space-orientation and kinesthetic-differentiation sbility. Plyometry. Stretching. **Afternoon**: Development of speed abilities and endurance in explosiveness. Game – football, basketball, „debla".	20 min. Sport game, 15 min. Gymnastic warm-up, 5x10 repetitions for each coordination ability. 6-8 exercises 2x10 repetitions each, 10-15 min. Game.
Thursday	**Morning**: Development of coordination abilities with the focus on kinesthetic-differentiation ability. Game: 3-3, 4-4. Flexibility and compensation exercises.	6-8 exercises 3x10 repetitions for each coordination ability. 30 min.
Friday	**Morning**: Development of coordination and strength abilities. Focus: kinesthetic-differentiation and space-orientation ability. Strength exercises – circular form. Dynamic strength of arms – medicine balls, rubber expanders – contrast method. **Afternoon**: Development of speed frequency and reaction speed. Reaction exercises with the change of direction of the movement. Flexibility and compensation exercises.	10-15 min. Gymnastic warm-up 6-8 exercises 3x10 repetitions each 25 min. 8-10 stands – 10-15 repetitions 30 min. 15 min.
Saturday	Development of aerobic endurance – continuous steady running in the nature.	20-30 min.

Conclusion

The work presented here contributes to elaborating on the selection of suitable content for sport preparation in the initial stages of volleyball training with a focus on the development of coordination abilities. We based this elaboration on a thorough analysis and generalized knowledge and experiences of experts in the sphere of modelling and planning sport preparation, as well as on theories of coordination abilities. Modern knowledge supports the view that the development of coordination abilities should become an inseparable part of sport preparation in each sport game.

The model of the development of coordination abilities limiting sport performance in volleyball presented here is recommended for application in the preparatory and partially also in the main, competitive period, in initial stages of sport preparation. The selection of talented individuals in practice is often realized in the form of recruiting instead of selection. Testing of conditional factors at the age of 10 years cannot exactly disclose the level of coordination abilities, which play an important role mostly in initial stages of sport preparation. We offer to coaches diagnostic means for the assessment and selection of talented individuals into sport classes, sport clubs and units, since these should not be based barely on finding out conditioning factors, somatic and psychic prerequisites for sport performance, but also on a thorough knowledge of the level of coordination abilities.

Consistent application of the submitted model of development of coordination abilities should contribute to a faster acquisition and improvement of motor skills, improvement of motor performance of athletes as well as higher effectiveness of a player in a sport game.

© 2014 Jaromír Šimonek
This work is licensed under the Creative Commons Attribution-NonCommercial-NoDerivs 3.0 License.

References

Antoniewicz, A., & Šimonek, J. (1998). Influence of the development of motor abilities of boys specializing in ice-hockey on the game performance. In: *Rocznik Naukowy-Yearbook*. Biala Podlaska: Jurgraf, vol.5, pp. 5-9.

Barber-Westin, S.D., Noyes, F.R., & Galloway, M. (2006). Jump-land characteristics and muscle strength development in young athletes, *American Journal of Sports Medicine, 34*(3): 375-384.

Baumann, H., & Reim, H. (1989). *Bewegungslehre*. Frankfurt: Eigenverlag.

Bekkering, H., & Sailer, U. (2002). Commentary: coordination of eye and hand in time and space. *Progress in Brain Research 140*: 365-373.

Belej, M. (1989). Možnosti zvyšovania účinnosti motorického učenia v Tv procese. In: *Progresívne trendy výučby v Tv procese*. Zborník Prešov: UPJŠ, pp. 106-119.

Belej, M., Starosta, W., Bajdzinski, M., Kos, A., Debczyňska, I. & Radziňska, M. (1994). Coordination skills in pupils between ages 11 – 14 in Prešov. *Telesná Výchova a Šport, 4*(1): 15-17.

Belej, M., & Starosta, W. (1994). Standards and norms of conditional and coordination skills in pupils between the ages 11 – 14 in Prešov (Slovakia). *Sport Kinetics. Third International Conference*, Poznaň, pp. 75-84.

Belej, M., Junger, J., & Feč. R. (1997). Dynamism of development of coordination skills in children between the ages of 5 – 14 from Prešov. In: *3rd International Symposium Sport of the Young*. Bled: Slovenija, pp. 70-73.

Belej, M. (1999). Rozvoj koordinačných schopností detí mladšieho a stredného školského veku. In: *Zborník výstupov z grantovej úlohy 1/1388/94. Identifikácia a rozvoj pohybových schopností detí a mládeže*. Prešov: FHPV PU, pp. 75-82.

Bloomfield, J.R., Polman, R., O'Donoghue, P. & McNaughton, L. (2007). Effective speed and agility conditioning methodology for random intermittent dynamic type of sports. *Journal of Strength and Conditioning Research, 21*: 1093-1100.

Blume, D.D. (1978). Zu einigen wesentlichen theoretischen Grundpositionen fur die Untersuchung der koordinativen Fähigkeiten. *Theorie und Praxis der Körperkult., 27*(1): 29-36.

Blume, D.D. (1981). Kennzeichnung koordinativer Fähigkeiten und Möglichkeiten ihrer Herausbildung in Trainingsprozess. *Wissenschaftliche Zeitschrift, 22*(3): 17-41.

Blume, D.D., & Hobusch, P. (1982). Koordinative Fähigkeiten – auch im Tennis wichtige Leistungsvoraussetzung. *Wissenschaftliche Zeitschrift, 22*(3): 43-56.

Bompa, T. (1999). *Periodization training for sports*. Champaign, Human Kinetics.

Bompa, T. (2000). *Total training for young champions,* Champaign, IL: Human Kinetics.

Bös, K., & Mechling, H. (1983). *Dimensionen sportmotorischer Leistungen*. Schorndorf: Verlag Hoffmann.

Brandt, C. (1979). Entwicklung der visuellen Orientierungsfähigkeit bei Volleyballspielern. *Theorie und Praxis der Körperkultur(Berlin),28*(2): 114-117.

Brandt, C. (1985). Entwicklung koordinativen Fähigkeiten im Volleyballtraining. *Theorie und Praxis der Körperkultur, 34*(4): 268.

Bressel, E., Yonker, J.C., Kras, J., & Heath, E.M. (2007). Comparison of static and dynamic balance in female collegiate soccer, basketball and gymnastic athletes, *Journal of Athletic Training, 42*(1): 42-46.

Čechov, O.S. (1979). *Osnovy volejbola*. Moskva: FiS, 1979.
Dannemann, F. (1982). Das Koordinationstraining für den Volleyball-Spieler: *Lehre und Praxis Volleyball, 9*(2): 34-35.
Derka, G., Gottschling, C., & Kunz, M. (1995). Die 50 besten Sportarten. Erste umfessende Studie über die Top-Disziplinen: Fitness und Gesundheit ohne Umweltschäden. *Focus, das moderne Nachrichtenmagazin, 38*: 203-210.
Diaczuk, D. (1994). Zdolnośći koordynacyjne w pilce recznej w swietle dymorfizmu plciowego. In: Proceedings of the conference: *"Problemy dymorfizmu plciowego w sporcie"*. Katowice: AWF, pp. 275 – 283.
Dobrý, L. (1982). Vztah senzoricko-motorických dovedností a koordinačních schopností ako primární podmínka výkonnostní úrovně hráče. In: *Koordinační schopnosti a pohybové dovednosti*. Metodický dopis. Praha: ÚV ČSTV. 168-173.
Doležajová, L. (1993). Príklady cvičení na rozvoj koordinačných schopností. *Telesná Výchova a Šport, 3*(1): 23-25.
Doležajová, L., Melišová, L., Šimonek, J., & Zaťková, V. (1995). Rozvoj koordinačných schopností v športovej príprave. In: *Acta Facultatis Educationis Physicae Universitatis Comenianae, XXXVI*. Bratislava: UK, pp. 105-112.
Dovalil, J., Choutka, M., Svoboda, B., Hošek, V., Perič, T., Potměšil, J., Vránová, J., & Bunc, V. (2002). *Výkon a trénink ve sportu*. Praha: Olympia.
Etzold, R. (1973). Technik – Fertigkeit. *Körpererziehung 23*:11.
Feč, K. (1992). Vzťah úrovne pohybovej koordinácie a výkonnosti na II. stupni ZŠ. In: *Zborník z 2. ved. seminára*. Prešov: VSTŠ, pp. 106-15.
Feč, K., Junger, J., & Belej, M. (1995). Entwicklung der motorischen Koordination und kinesteticdifferenzierenden Fähigkeit von 5-8 Jährigen Kindern. In: *Science in sports team games*. Biala Podlaska: Poland, pp. 532-536.
Felix, K. (1997). *Základy teórie športového tréningu*. Nitra: UKF.
Frömel, K. (1982). Současné učební postupy při osvojování tělovýchovných dovedností. In: Měkota, K.: *Koordinační schopnosti a pohybová dovednost*. Metodický dopis. Praha: ÚV ČSTV, pp. 179-185.
Gabbett, T.J., Kelly, J.N., & Sheppard, J.M. (2008). Speed, change of direction speed, and reactive agility of rugby league players. *Journal of Strength and Conditioning Research, 22*: 174-181.
Gabriel, S. (1991). Das Training der koordinativer Fähigkeiten im F- bis D- Jugendalter. *Fussballtraining, 9*(11): 27-34.
Gamble, P. (2013). *Strength and conditioning for team sports*. (Sport Specific Physical Preparation for High Performance). Routledge Taylor and Francis Group. 2nd ed.
Gerhát, Š., Kollárovits, Z., & Teplická, S. (1995). Bisexuálna dymorfnosť v ukazovateľoch kinesteticko-diferenciačných schopností 6-17-ročnej mládeže. *Telesná Výchova a Šport, 5*(4): 12-16.
Górska, K., & Gierat, B. (1995). Zróżnicowanie plciowe rozwoju koordynacyjnych zdolności motorycznych u dzieci w wieku 11-13 lat. In: *Zborník z konferencie"Problemy dymorfizmu plciowego w sporcie (cz.2)*. Katowice, pp. 203-209.
Halmová, N. (2000). Úroveň a rozvoj koordinačných schopností u detí predškolského veku. In: *Zborník z III. Medzinárodnej konferencie v Nitre*. Nitra: SVS pre TVŠ, pp. 65-69.

Hartmann, Ch. (1992). Diagnose und das Training koordinativer Fähigkeiten unter handlungsorientierter Sicht. In: *Leipziger Sportwissenschaftliche Beiträge, 33*,(1): 7-13.

Havlíček, I. (1998). Metodologické prístupy k skúmaniu štruktúry športového výkonu. *Telesná Výchova a Šport,* 8(1): 5-8.

Heinzel, A., Koch, P., & Strakerjahn U. (1997). *Koordinationstraining im Tennis.* Sindelfingen: Sportverlag Schmidt & Dreisilker.

Herzog, P., Voigt, H.F., & Westfahel, H. (1985). *Volleyballtraining*, 1985. 87 p.

Healthofchildren.com. (2013). [online] 2013. [Retrieved on August 15, 2013]. Available online at:<http://www.healthofchildren.com/G-H/Hand-Eye-oordination. html#ixzz2eTWZ lO60>.

Healthofchildren.com. (2013). [online] 2013. [Retrieved on June 15, 2013]. Available online at:<http://www.healthofchildren.com/G-H/Hand-Eye-Coordination.html#ixzz2e TXIu1Xi>.

Hirtz, P. (1977). Struktur und Entwicklung koordinativer Leistungsvoraussetzungen bei Schulkindern. *Theorie und Praxis der Körperkultur (Berlin), 26*(7): 503-510.

Hirtz, P. (1981). Koordinative Fähigkeiten – Kennzeichnung, Alternsgang und Beeinflussungsmöglichkeiten. In: *Medizin und Sport, 21*(11): 348-351.

Hirtz, P. (1985). *Koordinative Fähigkeiten im Schulsport.* Berlin: Volk und Wissen Volkseigener Verlag.

Holtz, D. (1977). Die Entwicklung der Rhytmusfähigkeit bei Schulkindern. *Theorie und Praxis der Körperkult.* 26(7): 523-526.

Choutka, M., & Dovalil, J. (1991). *Sportovní trénink.* Praha: Olympia.

Chovanová, E. (2000). Cieľavedomý rozvoj vybraných koordinačných schopností u detí mladšieho školského veku. In: *Zborník z medzinárodnej konferencie č.5.* Prešov: Vsl. Pobočka SVSTVŠ, pp. 192-195.

Israel, S. (1977). Bewegungskoordination frühzeitig ausbilden. *Leichtathlet, 28*: 989-992.

Ivojlov, A.V. (1984). *Volleyball – Biomechanik und Methodik.* Berlin: Sportverlag.

Jonath, V., & Krempel, R. (1991). *Konditionstraining.* Reinbeck bei Hamburg: Rewolt Sport Rororo.

Junger, J., & Turek, M. (1997). Telesný rozvoj a pohybová výkonnosť detí predškolského veku a mladšieho školského veku. In: *Zborník č.4„Telesný rozvoj a pohybová výkonnosť detí a mládeže".* Prešov: Vsl. Pobočka VSTVŠ, pp. 56-59.

Juřinová, I. (1982). Ontogeneze koordinačních schopností. In: Měkota, K.: *Koordinační schopnosti a pohybové dovednosti.* Metodický dopis. Praha: ÚV ČSTV.

Kampmiller, T. (1991). Osobitosti športovej prípravy detí a mládeže v atletike. In: Koštial, J. et al.: *Atletika – Zvolený šport.* Bratislava: Univerzita Komenského, pp. 82-84.

Kasa, J. (1991). *Pohybová činnosť v telesnej kultúre.* Bratislava, UK.

Kasa, J., & Feč., K. (1996). Porovnávací výskum úrovne koordinačných schopností na Slovensku. In: *Tělesná výchova a sport na přelomu století.* Praha: UK, pp. 480-483.

Kasa, J., & Šimonek, J. (1999). *Diagnostika a rozvoj koordinačných schopností.* Metodická príručka. Bratislava: Metodické centrum mesta Bratislava.

Kasa, J. (2000). *Športová antropomotorika.* Bratislava: UK. 209 p.

Kirchem, A. (1992). *Diagnostik motorischer Fähigkeiten und Auswirkungen einer Forderung der Bewegungskoordination im ausserunterrichtlichen Schulsport.* Erlensee: SFT-Verlag.

Klimin, V.P., & Koloskov, V.I. (1982). *Upravlenije podgotovki chokkejistov*. Moskva: FiS.

Koch, W. (1986). *Fussball – Handbuch für den übungsleiter*. Berlin: Sportverlag.

Kohoutek, M., Hendl, J., Véle, F., & Hirtz, P. (2005). *Koordinační schopnosti dětí. Výsledky čtyřletého longitudinálního sledování dětí ve věku 8-11 let*. Praha: Univerzita Karlova v Praze, Fakulta tělesné výchovy a sportu.

Kollárovits, Z., & Gerhát, Š. (1993). Hodnotenie kinesteticko-diferenciačných schopností. *Telesná Výchova a Šport, 3*(1): 14-18.

Kraemer, W.J., & Fleck, S.J. (2005). *Strength training for young athletes* (2nd Edition). Champaign, IL: Human Kinetics.

Krauspe, D., Malorny, S., & Rieck, I. (1986). Theoretische und Metodische Positionen zur Ausbildung koordinativer Fähigkeiten im Fussballsport. *Wiss. Zeitschrift der DHfK Leipzig, 27*(2): 32-49.

Letzelter, M. (1978). *Trainingsgrundlagen – Volleyball*. Reinbeck bei Hamburg: Rewolt Sport Rororo.

Little, T., & Williams, A.G. (2005). Specificity of acceleration, maximum speed, and agility in professional soccer players. *Journal of Strength and Conditioning Research, 19*: 76-78.

Ljach, V.I. (1988). Važnejšije dlja rozličnych vidov sporta koordynacyjnyje sposobnosti i ich značimosť v techničeskom i techniko-taktičeskom soveršenstvovanji. *Teoria i Praktika Fizičeskoj Kultury6*(2): 56-58.

Ljach, V.I. (1989). *Koordynacijonnyje sposobnosti škoľnikov*. Moskva: Polymija.

Ljach, V.I. (1990). *Razvitije koordinacionnych spasobnostej u detej škoľnovo vozrasta*. Moskva: FiS.

Ljach, V.I., Mynarski, W., & Raczek, J. (1995). Biopsychiczne predyspozycje koordynacyjnych zdolności motorycznych – przeglad badań w piśmiennictwie rosyjskojezycznym. *Antropomotoryka 12*: 83-103.

Ludwig, G. (1981). Ergebnisse eines pädagogischen Experiments zur koordinativen Vervollkomnung in Sportunterricht der Unterstufe. In: *Koordinative Fähigkeiten*. Greifswald: FMA Universität, pp. 56-61.

Mangi, R., Jokl, P., & Dayton, A.W. (1987). *Sports fitness and training*. New York: Pantheon Books.

Martin, D. (1981). Konzeption eines Modells für das Kinder- und Jugendtraining. *Leistungssport, (Frankfurt/M.), 11*(3): 165-176.

Martin, D. (1988). *Training im Kindes- und Jugendalter*. Schorndorf: Hoffmann–Verlag.

Meier, H.W. (1983). Charakteristik und Ausbildung der koordinativer Fähigkeiten im Fussballsport. *Theorie und Praxis der Körperkult. (Berlin), 32*(6): 537-541.

Melišová, L. (1995). Rozvoj koordinačných schopností v tenise. In: *Acta Facultatis Educationis Physicae Universitatis Comenianae, XXXVII*, Bratislava: UK, pp. 197-203.

Měkota, K. (1982). *Koordinační schopnosti a pohybové dovednosti*. Metodický dopis. Praha: VMO ÚV ČSTV.

Měkota, K., & Blahuš, P. (1983). *Motorické testy v tělesné výchově*. Praha: SPN.

Měkota, K., Kovář. R., Chytráčková, J., Gajda, V., Kohoutek, M., & Moravec, R. (1995). *UNIFITTEST (6-60). Tests and norms of motor performance and physical fitness in youth and in adult age*. Olomouc: VÚP.

Měkota, K. (2000). Definice a struktura motorických schopností (novější poznatky a střety názorů). In: *Česká kinantropologie, 4*(1): 59-69.

Miller, T. (2012). *NSCA´s guide to tests and assessments*. Human Kinetics. National strength and conditioning association. 357 p.

Moravec, R. (1990). *Telesný, funkčný rozvoj a pohybová výkonnosť 7-18-ročnej mládeže v ČSFR*. Bratislava: Šport.

Moravec, R., Kampmiller, T., Sedláček, J. Ramacsay, L., Slamka, M., Šimonek, J., & Čillík, I.. (1996). *Eurofit – telesný vývoj a pohybová výkonnosť školskej populácie*. Topoľčianky: End.

Moreno, E. (1995). Developing quickness, part II. *Strength and Conditioning Journal 17*: 38-39.

Mynarski, W, Raczek, J., & Ljach, V.I. (1998). Teoretyczno-empiryczne podstawy kstaltowania i diagnozowania koordynacyjnych zdolnosci motorycznych. *Studia nad motorycznosc ludzka 4*, Katowice: AWF.

Mynarski, W., & Prus, G. (1998). *Przydatnosc róznych form ruchowych w kszaltowaniu koordynacyjnych zdolnosci motorycznych*. Roczniky Naukowe. Katowice: AWF.

Nabatnikovova, M. J. (1982). *Osnovy upravlenija podgotovkoj junych athletesov*. Moskva: FiS.

Naughton, G., Farpour-Lambert, N.J., Carlson, J., Bradley, M., & van Praagh, E. (2000). Physiological issues surrounding the performance of adolescent athletes, *Sports Medicine, 30*(5): 309-325.

Neiling, W.D. (1992). Trainingsmittel zur Entwicklung koordinativer Fähigkeiten. *Handballtraining*, (Münster) *14*(6): 17-23.

Nicklisch, R., & Zimmermann, K. (1981). Die Ausbildung koordinativer Fähigkeiten und ihre Bedeutung für die technische beziehungsweise technisch-taktische Leistungsfähigkeit der Sportler. *Theorie und Praxis der Körperkultur. (Berlin), 30*(10): 764-768.

Nishijima, T., Ohsawa, S., & Matsuura, Y. (1987). The relationship between the game performance and group skill in volleyball. *International Journal of Physical Education (Schorndorf, FRG) 24*(4): 20-26.

Osiński, W. (1993). *Motoryczność czlowieka – jej struktura, zmienność i uwarunkowania*. Poznaň: AWF.

Peráček, P. (1995). *Futbal. Riadenie – plánovanie – tréning*. Bratislava: P. Mačura.

Philippaerts, R.M., Vaeyens, R., Janssens, M., Van Renterghem, B., Matthys, D., Craen, R, Bourgois, J, Vrijens, J., Beunen, G., & Malina R.M. (2006). The relationship between peak height velocity and physical performance in youth soccer players, *Journal of Sports Sciences, 24*(3): 221-230.

Plisk, S.S. (2008). Speed, agility, and speed-endurance development. In: *Essentials of strength training and conditioning*. T.R. Baechle and R.W. Earle, eds. Champaign, IL: Human Kinetics.

Przeweda, R., & Trzesniowski, R. (1992). Przemiany sprawnosci fizycznej mlodziezy w Polsce. *Wychowanie Fizyczne i Sport, 4:* 3-15.

Quatman, C.E., Ford, K.R., Myer, G.D., & Hewett, T.E. (2006). Maturation leads to gender differences in landing force and vertical jump performance, *American Journal of Sports Medicine, 34*(5): 806-813.

Raczek, J. (1990). Koordinativ-motorische Vervollkomnung und sportmotorische Lehrnerfol-ge im Sportunterricht und Nachwuchstraining. *Leistungssport, 20*(5): 4-9.

Raczek, J., & Mynarski, W. (1991). Zmienność ontogenetyczna wybranych koordynacyjnych zdolnośći motorycznych dzieci i mlodziezi w wieku 7-18 lat. *Antropomotoryka, 3*(6).

Raczek, J., &. Mynarski, W. (1992). *Koordynacyjne zdolnosci motoryczne dzieci i mlodziezy. Studia nad motorycznoscia ludska*. Katowice: AWF.

Račev, K. (1978). *Iz opita na trenora.* Sofia: Medicina i fizkultura.

Rieder, H., Bös, K., Reischle, K., & *Mechling*, H. (1983). *Motorik und Bewegungsforschung. Ein Beitrag zum Lernen im Sport.* Schorndorf: Hoffmann Verlag.

Riegerová, J., & Ulbrichová, M. (1998). *Aplikace fyzické antropologie v tělesné výchově a sportu.* Olomouc: Vydavatelství University Palackého.

Rostock, J. (1982). Zur Ausprägung sportlicher Fertigkeiten im Schulsport unter koordinationstheoretischer Sicht.*Teorie und Praxis der Körperkultur 31*(8): 626-630.

Roth, K. (1982). *Strukturanalyse koordinativer Fähigkeiten.* Bad Homburg: Limpert Verlag.

Rutkowska, M., & Kucharska, A. (1987). *The levels of coordination of the movement tested on 10-year-old girls.* Biology of Sport (Warszaw), 4(3-4): 141-146.

Rousseau, R. (2013). *How to Improve Hand Eye Coordination.* [online] 2013. [Retrieved on September 9, 2013]. Available online at:<http://www.bodyomics.com/ articles/hand_eye_coor dination.html>.

Schmid, H. (1984). Sprunggewandtheit als Trainingsziel. *Lehre und Praxis des Volleyballspiels, 3*: 28-29.

Schmidt, R.A., & Lee, T.D. (2011). *Motor control and learning.* 5th Edition: A Behavioral Emphasis. Los Angeles: Mc. Master University USA. Human Kinetics Book.

Schnabel, G., & Thiess, G. (1993). *Lexikon Sport Wissenschaft. Berlin.* Sport und Gesundheit Verlag.

Schnabel, G., Harre, D., & Borde, A. (1994). *Trainingswissenschaft.* Berlin, Sportverlag.

Schnabel, G., Harre, D., & Borde, A. (1997). *Trainingswissenschaft: Leistung - Training –Wettkampf.* Berlin : SVB Sportverlag.

Schneider, H. (1992). Koordinative Fähigkeiten im Tennis – Möglichkeiten ihrer Verbesserung und Schulung. *Sportunterricht, 7*: 105-111.

Sehlbach, U. (1988). *Leistungsdiagnostik in der Talentsuche und Talentforderung.* Dissertation. Dortmund.

Serpell, B.G., Young, W.B., & Ford, M. (2011). Are the perceptual and decision-making aspects of agility trainable? A preliminary investigation. *Journal of Strength and Conditioning Research,* 25(5): 1240-1248.

Sheppard, J.M., & Young, W.B (2006). Agility literature review: classifications, training and testing. *Journal of Sports Sciences 24*: 919-932.

Šimonek, J., Herrmann, G., Prieložný, I., Rehák, M., Starší, J., & Vengloš, J. (1987). *Kondičná príprava v kolektívnych športových hrách.* Bratislava: Šport STV.

Šimonek, J., & Zrubák, A. (1995). *Základy kondičnej prípravy v športe.* Bratislava: UK.

Šimonek, J. (1993). Prostriedky rozvoja koordinačných schopností mladých volejbalistov. *Telesná Výchova a Šport, 3*(1): 26-29.

Šimonek, J. (1994). The development of coordination abilities in volleyball players of younger school age. In: *Magazine of Scientific Society of Physical Education and Sport II.* Bratislava: Vedecká spoločnosť pre TVŠ, pp. 61-65.

Šimonek, J. (1995). De ontwikkeling van koordinatievaardigheden bij jonge volleyballers. *Volley Magazine 23*(11): 10-12.

Šimonek, J., Šutka, V., Halmová, N., Antoniewicz, A., Polóny, J. & Baráth, L.. (1997). Monitorovanie úrovne koordinačných schopností školskej populácie vo veku 10-17 rokov. *Telesná Výchova a Šport, 7*(1): 17-21.

Šimonek, J. (1998). *Hodnotenie a rozvoj koordinačných schopností 10-17-ročných chlapcov a dievčat*. Nitra: Univerzita Konštantína Filozofa.

Šimonek, J., Halmová, N., Klárová, R., Gyetvai, G., & Szatmári, Z. (2000). Studies on the level of distance estimation ability in 6-22-year-old population in the Central European region. In: *Studia Kinantropologia, 1*(1): 187-191.

Šimonek, J. (2013a). Niekoľko poznámok k chápaniu pojmu agilita. *Telesná Výchova a Šport, 23*(1): 18-23.

Šimonek, J. (2013b). Development of speed and coordination by means of agility training at school P.E. lessons In: *Current trends in educational science and practice III. International proceedings of scientific studies*. Radmila Nikolič (ed.). Užice: Teachers´ Training Faculty, pp. 129-135.

Singer, R.N. (1985). *Motor learning and human performance*. New York: McMillan Publishers.

Starosta, W. (1984). Movement coordination as an element in sport selection system. *Biology of Sport, Warszaw, 1*(2): 139-153.

Starosta, W., & Hirtz, P. (1989). Sensitive and critical periods in development of coordination abilities in children and youth. *Biology of Sport, Supplement 3, 6*: 276-282.

Starosta, W. (1995). Koordinations und Konditionsfähigkeiten bei Mannschaftsspielen. In: *Science in Sports Team Games*. J. Bergier (ed.) Academy of Physical Education, Biala Podlaska: IASK, 69-104.

Starosta, W. (2003). *Motoryczne zdolnosci koordynacyjne. Znaczenie, struktura, uwarunkowania, kstaltowanie*. Warszawa:Miedzynarodowe stowarzysenie motoryki sportowej, 2003. 568 p.

Sýkora, F., Šimonek, J., Kasa, J., Macák, I., Hrčka, F., & Korček, F. (1995). *Telesná výchova a šport*. Terminologický a výkladový slovník. Bratislava: F. R. and G. spol. s r.o., 402 p.

Szczepanik, M. (1993). Wplyw treningu koordynacijnego na szybkosc uczenia sie techniki ruchu w siatkowce. *Sport Wyczynowy, 3*(4): 41-51.

Szczepanik, M., & Szopa, J. (1993). *Wplyw ukierunkowanego treningu na rozwoj predyspozycji koordynacyjnych oraz szybkości uczenia sie techniki ruchu u mlodych siatkarzy*. Wydawnictwa Monograficzne 54, Krakow, AWF.

Topcondition.com. (2013). Activities for infants which develop hand eye and hand foot coordination. A Fit Tot. [Retrieved on July 29, 2013].
    Available online at:< http://www.topcondition.com/temp/ Afittot/hand_eyecoordina tion. htm>.

Trzesniowski, R. (1990). *Rozwoj fizyczny i sprawnosc fizyczna mlodziezy skolnej w Polsce*. Warszawa: AWF.

Trzesniowski, R., &. Pilicz, S. (1989). *Tabele sprawnosci fizycznej mlodziezy w wieku 7-19 lat*. Warszawa: AWF.

Turek, M. (1998). Prognózovanie a modelovanie v športe. In: *Antropomotorika*. Zborník referátov zo seminára učiteľov antropomotoriky SR a ČR. Donovaly: VSTVŠ, KTVŠ FHV UMB v Banskej Bystrici a ČVS Kinantropologie, pp. 75-81.

Vanhille, L. (1992). *Handig met de bal*. Brussel: NSVO Schoolsport.

Vojčík, M., Šimonek, J., Brtkova, M., Argaj, G., Bebčáková, V., Mačura, P., & Trnovský, I. (1997). *Basketbal komplexne*. Bratislava: SBA.

Young, W.B., James, R., & Montgomery, I. (2002). Is muscle power related to running speed with changes of direction? *Journal of Sports Medicine and Physical Fitness 42*: 282-288.

Zaciorskij, V. (1979). Kibernetika i sport. In *Programirovannoje obučenije i primenenije techničeskich sredstv v sportivnoj trenirovke*. Minsk: Polymja.

Zaťková, V. (1993). Vplyv vybraných cvičení na rozvoj koordinačných schopností v hádzanej. *Telesná Výchova a Šport, 3*(1): 19-23.

Zháněl, J., & Zlesák, F. (1999). *Koordinační schopnosti v tenise (Přehled, význam a rozvoj)*. Olomouc: UP.

Ziegenhagen, U. (1992). Koordinations-programme. *Handballtraining, 10:* 23-27.

Zimmer, H. (1986). Zur Struktur Koordinativer Fähigkeiten und zu Möglichkeiten ihrer Erfassung. *Wiss. Zeitschrift der DHfK Leipzig, 27*(1): 90-112.

Zimmermann, K., & Nicklisch, R. (1981). Die Ausbildung koordinativer Fähigkeiten und ihre Bedeutung für die technische bzw. Technisch-taktische Leistungsfähigkeit der Sportler. *Theorie und Praxis der Körperkult. (Berlin),30*(10): 764-768.

Zimmermann, K. (1982). Wesentliche koordinative Fähigkeiten für Sportspiele. *Theorie und Praxis der Körperkult. (Berlin), 31*(6): 439-443.

Zimmermann, K. (1983). Zur Weiterentwicklung der Theorie der koordinativen Fähigkeiten. *Wissenschaftliche Zeitschrift, 3*: 33-44.

Zimmermann, K., Pohle, H., & Kallenbach, U. (1987). Testprofil zur Erfassung ausgewählter koordinativer Fähigkeiten im Handball. *Theorie und Praxis der Körperkultur (Berlin), 36*(2): 112-116.

Žak, S. (1991). *Zdolnosci kondycyjne i koordynacyjnyje dzieci i mlodziezy z populacji wielkomiejskiej na tle wybranych uwarunkowan somatycznych i aktywnosci ruchowej*. Krakow: AWF.

Zeleznjak, J.D. (1988). *Junyj volejbolist*. Moskva: FiS.

Index

Acquisition of skills 69
Adaptation 4, 9, 14, 21, 33, 50
Age dynamism 3-4
Agility 5-6, 19, 24-25, 36, 55, 72-73, 75-78
Analysers 3-4, 14, 18, 20, 30, 32, 40
Anticipation 14, 50, 54
Balance ability 5, 24, 29, 43, 53
Behaviour 2, 4, 14
Bench walk with 3 turns 44
Biological age 10
Blocker 55, 57
Central nervous system 4, 14, 18
Competitive period 8, 71
Conditioning 1, 3, 8-9, 11-12, 17, 20-21, 25, 28, 33, 42-43, 49-50, 58, 71-73, 75-77
Conditioning load 28
Coordination 1, 3-12, 14, 16-72, 77-78
Coordination abilities 1, 5-6, 8-11, 16-54, 56-71, 77-78
Coordination preparation 1, 3, 7, 9-10, 12, 17, 30, 49, 58, 60, 69
Coordination test 42
Coupling 5, 53
Developmental peculiarities 2
Distance estimation 37-38, 78
Dynamic balance 6, 14, 23-24, 36, 40-41, 72
Effectiveness 1, 5, 7, 21, 23, 30-31, 49, 69, 71
Eye-hand coordination 7, 23
Feeling of ball 55
Fitness 10, 17, 26, 73, 75, 78
Flamengo test 42
Functional preparedness 3-4, 13
Game activities 6, 10, 14, 24, 31, 53
Individual peculiarities 4
Kinesthetic-differentiation 5, 22-23, 26, 28-29, 36, 39, 44, 46-48, 52-53, 55, 60, 62-63
Limiting factors 7, 16
Long-term sports preparation 1-3
Maturation 10, 76

Medical observation 8
Model 1-4, 7, 12-13, 16-19, 49-52, 54, 56-58, 60, 62-64, 66, 68, 70-71
Modelling 1-3, 7, 9, 11, 58, 71
Motivation 13, 32, 56, 61-63
Motor abilities 2-4, 9, 13, 16-19, 21, 26-27, 33, 36, 39, 43, 72
Motor control 22, 50, 77
Motor learning 22, 26, 29, 36, 38, 78
Motor performance 1, 26, 42, 71, 75
Motor prerequisites 1, 8, 18, 41, 43, 50
Motor skills 1, 4-5, 7, 9-10, 13, 19, 21, 23, 25-28, 30, 32, 34, 36, 40, 49-50, 53, 60, 67, 71
Motor task 21, 36-37, 56
Movement control 4, 18, 27, 34, 47
Movement rhythm observation 46
Nervo-muscular processes 4, 18
Peculiarities 2, 4, 35, 37-39, 41
Performance standards 43-45, 47
Periodisation 10
Physical preparation 3, 8-11, 28, 50, 58, 60, 73
Prediction 3
Preparatory period 8, 10, 63, 70
Prerequisites 1, 3, 5, 7-9, 11-12, 14, 16, 18, 20-21, 25, 28, 30, 33, 36, 38, 41-44, 47, 49-50, 52, 71
Quickness 6, 25, 76
Rational sports technique 2
Reaction speed 5, 22, 26, 28-29, 32-33, 36, 39-40, 43, 50, 52-55, 60-61
Rhythmic ability 5, 23, 26, 29, 36, 39, 43, 53
Sensitive periods 1, 3, 28, 39
Sensomotoric coordination 14
Setter 52, 55-57, 68
Shuttle run 39, 46-47
Sitting target throw 39
Skeletal muscles 4, 18, 21
Skills acquisition 11, 26
Somatotype 20

Space-orientation ability 28-29, 39, 43, 47, 56, 67
Special conditioning 8-9
Speed 5-6, 10, 17-18, 20-22, 25-29, 32-34, 36, 39-40, 43, 47, 50, 52-55, 60-61, 67, 72-73, 75-76, 78
Speed-strength abilities 17, 40
Spiker 54-57
Sport form 4
Sport mastery 4, 9-10, 25, 40, 49
Sport performance 4, 7, 9, 12-14, 16-18, 20, 22, 24, 26-28, 30, 32, 36, 43, 48-49, 52-53, 55-58, 71
Sports games 1, 14, 24
Sports performance structure 3
Sports preparation 1-3, 12
Static balance 40, 42
Stopping the rolling ball 45
Tactical acting 4

Target sitting throw 46
Target standing broad jump 46
Technique 1-2, 5, 9, 11-12, 19, 21, 25-26, 28-29, 32, 34-35, 49, 57
Testing 1, 37, 42, 46, 71, 77
Time estimation 46-47
Top athlete 2
Top sport 1, 3, 12, 18, 44, 49, 56, 58, 69
Training load 57
Training means 2, 53
Training methods 30, 49
Training programme 59
Training units 1-2, 50, 60
Vestibular apparatus 5, 23
Vision 7, 23, 50
Volleyball 1, 3-4, 7-11, 17, 22-24, 26, 29, 31-34, 44, 47-71, 73-77
Youth training 10

www.ingramcontent.com/pod-product-compliance
Lightning Source LLC
Chambersburg PA
CBHW040122120426
42814CB00009B/340